Eyewitness
SKELETON

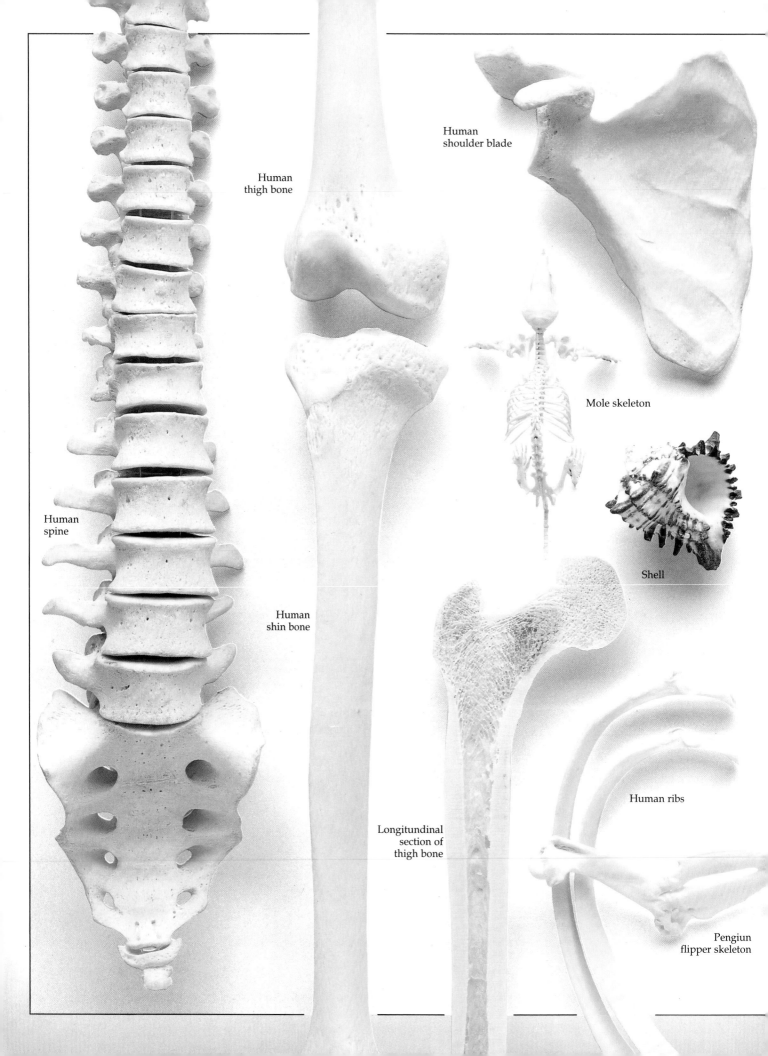

Human
thigh bone

Human
shoulder blade

Human
spine

Mole skeleton

Shell

Human
shin bone

Human ribs

Longitundinal
section of
thigh bone

Pengiun
flipper skeleton

Human
molars

Star shell

Eyewitness
SKELETON

In association with
THE NATURAL HISTORY MUSEUM

Written by
STEVE PARKER

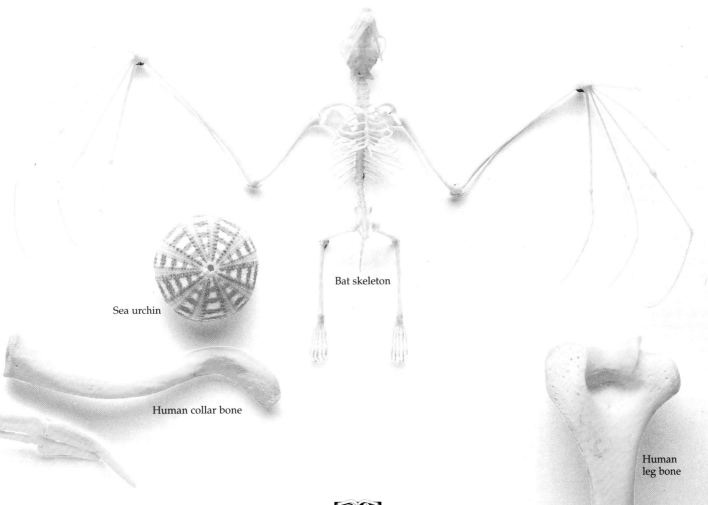

Sea urchin

Bat skeleton

Human collar bone

Human
leg bone

DK

Dorling Kindersley

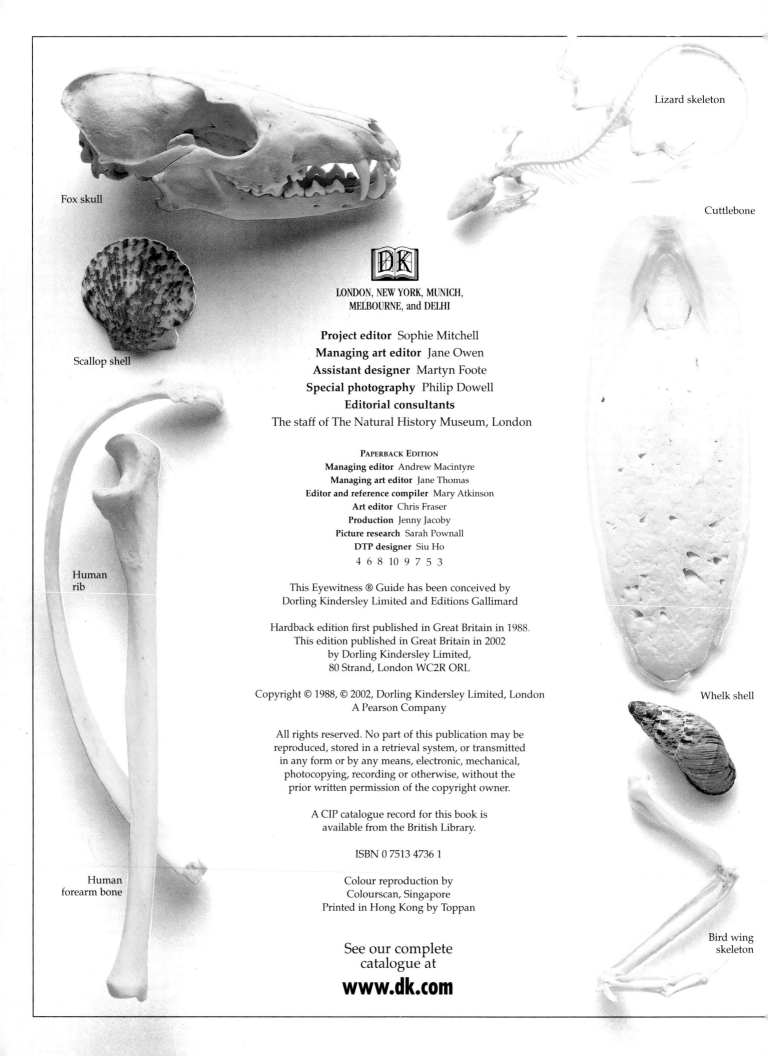

Fox skull

Lizard skeleton

Cuttlebone

Scallop shell

DK

LONDON, NEW YORK, MUNICH,
MELBOURNE, and DELHI

Project editor Sophie Mitchell
Managing art editor Jane Owen
Assistant designer Martyn Foote
Special photography Philip Dowell
Editorial consultants
The staff of The Natural History Museum, London

PAPERBACK EDITION
Managing editor Andrew Macintyre
Managing art editor Jane Thomas
Editor and reference compiler Mary Atkinson
Art editor Chris Fraser
Production Jenny Jacoby
Picture research Sarah Pownall
DTP designer Siu Ho
4 6 8 10 9 7 5 3

This Eyewitness ® Guide has been conceived by
Dorling Kindersley Limited and Editions Gallimard

Hardback edition first published in Great Britain in 1988.
This edition published in Great Britain in 2002
by Dorling Kindersley Limited,
80 Strand, London WC2R ORL

A CIP catalogue record for this book is
available from the British Library.

ISBN 0 7513 4736 1

Colour reproduction by
Colourscan, Singapore
Printed in Hong Kong by Toppan

See our complete
catalogue at
www.dk.com

Human
rib

Human
forearm bone

Whelk shell

Bird wing
skeleton

Contents

Crow skull

Parrot skull

The human skeleton

A SKELETON IS MANY THINGS: symbol of danger and death, a key that opens any door, a secret kept in a cupboard, the outline of a novel or grand plan . . . and the 200-odd bones that hold up each human body. Our skeleton supports, moves and protects. It is both rigid and flexible. Individual bones are stiff and unyielding, forming an internal framework that supports the rest of the body and stops it collapsing into a jelly-like heap. Bones together, linked by moveable joints and worked by muscles, form a system of girders, levers and pincers that can pick an apple from a tree or propel the whole body at 35 kph (20 mph). The skeleton protects our most delicate and vital organs: the skull shields the brain, and the ribs guard the heart and lungs. The human skeleton follows the basic design found in the 40,000 or so species of backboned animals. But the endless variety of animals has a correspondingly endless variety of skeletons, as this book sets out to show.

BIG HEAD
The human skull houses one of the biggest brains, in relation to body size, in the animal world (p. 26).

EARLY IMPRESSION *above*
Medical textbooks of the 18th and 19th centuries would have contained detailed illustrations such as this.

ANATOMY LECTURE *below*
A medieval lecture theatre populated by human and animal skeletons.

MEDIEVAL MEDICINE
The surgeon points out details of the rib cage to a 15th-century student.

FOOD PROCESSORS
Human teeth chop their way through about 500 kg (half a tonne) of food each year (p. 27).

MEASURING THE SKULL
The craniometer, a device for measuring skull size - and, by deduction, brain size.

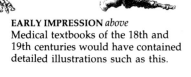

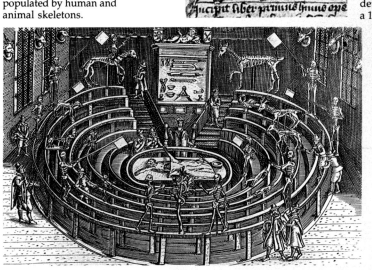

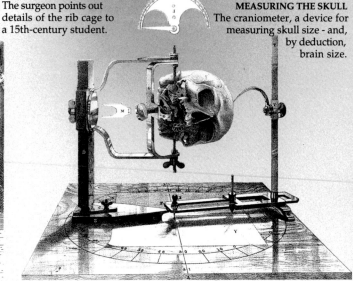

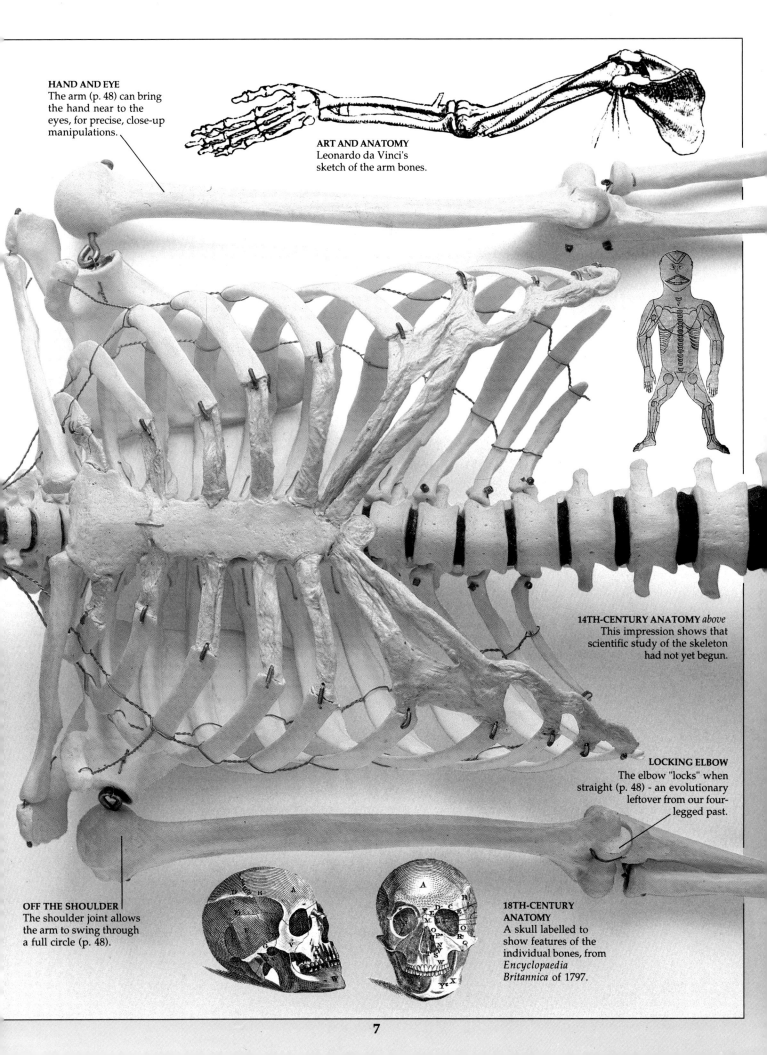

HAND AND EYE
The arm (p. 48) can bring the hand near to the eyes, for precise, close-up manipulations.

ART AND ANATOMY
Leonardo da Vinci's sketch of the arm bones.

14TH-CENTURY ANATOMY *above*
This impression shows that scientific study of the skeleton had not yet begun.

LOCKING ELBOW
The elbow "locks" when straight (p. 48) - an evolutionary leftover from our four-legged past.

OFF THE SHOULDER
The shoulder joint allows the arm to swing through a full circle (p. 48).

18TH-CENTURY ANATOMY
A skull labelled to show features of the individual bones, from *Encyclopaedia Britannica* of 1797.

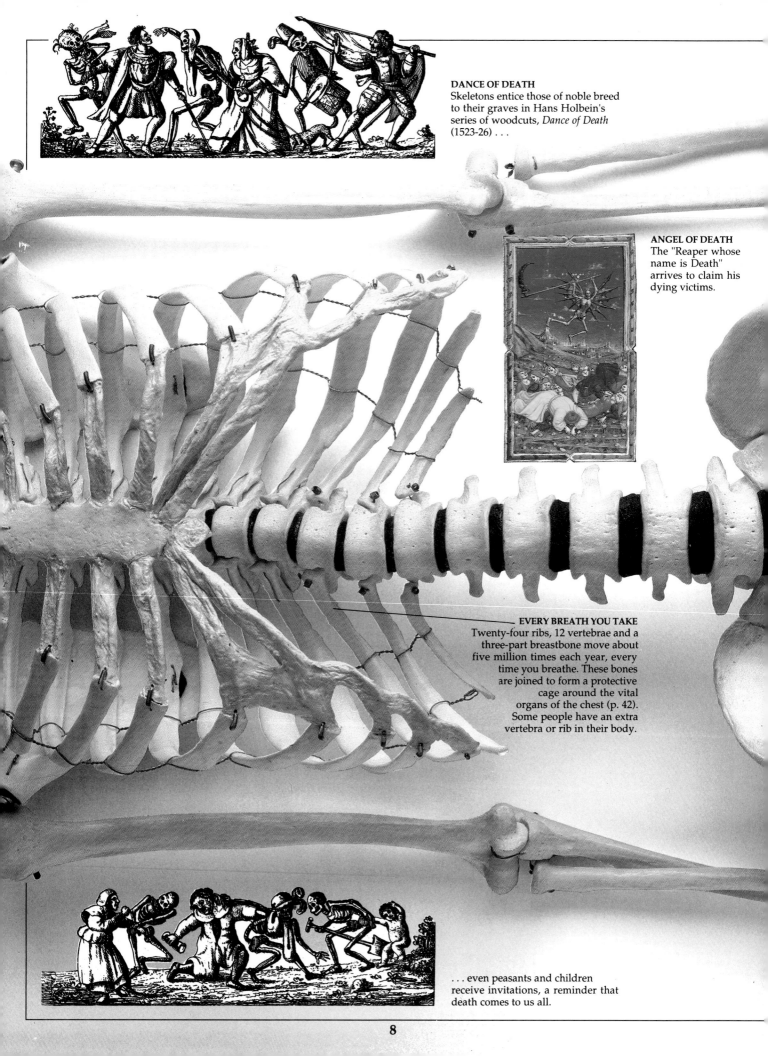

DANCE OF DEATH
Skeletons entice those of noble breed to their graves in Hans Holbein's series of woodcuts, *Dance of Death* (1523-26) . . .

ANGEL OF DEATH
The "Reaper whose name is Death" arrives to claim his dying victims.

EVERY BREATH YOU TAKE
Twenty-four ribs, 12 vertebrae and a three-part breastbone move about five million times each year, every time you breathe. These bones are joined to form a protective cage around the vital organs of the chest (p. 42). Some people have an extra vertebra or rib in their body.

. . . even peasants and children receive invitations, a reminder that death comes to us all.

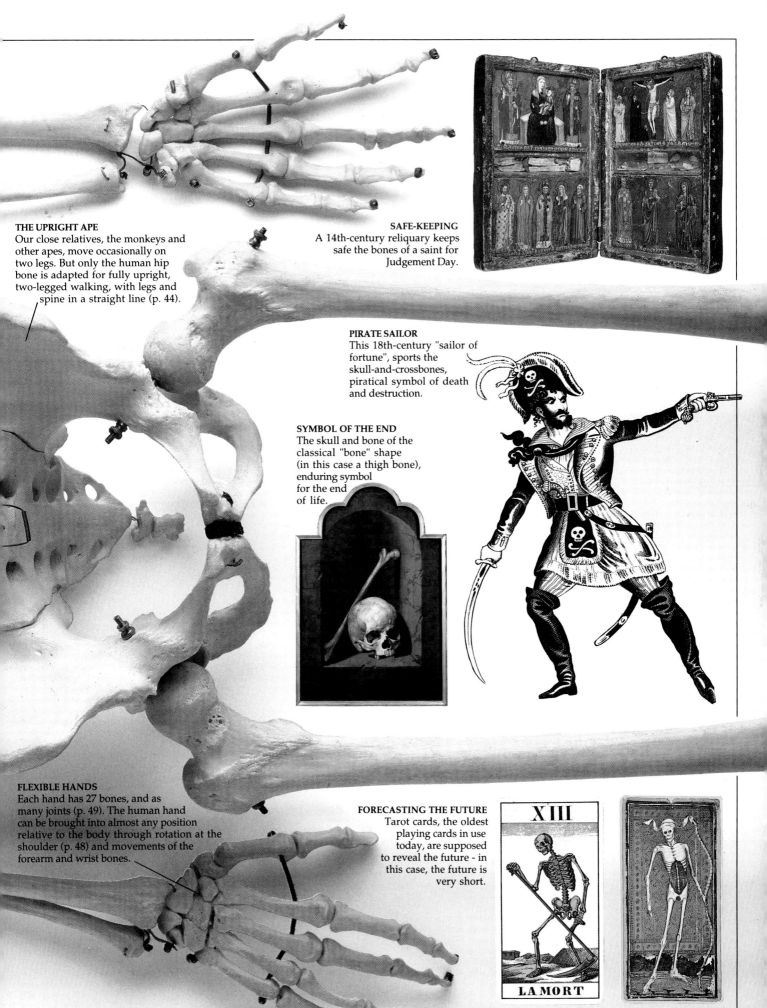

THE UPRIGHT APE
Our close relatives, the monkeys and other apes, move occasionally on two legs. But only the human hip bone is adapted for fully upright, two-legged walking, with legs and spine in a straight line (p. 44).

SAFE-KEEPING
A 14th-century reliquary keeps safe the bones of a saint for Judgement Day.

PIRATE SAILOR
This 18th-century "sailor of fortune", sports the skull-and-crossbones, piratical symbol of death and destruction.

SYMBOL OF THE END
The skull and bone of the classical "bone" shape (in this case a thigh bone), enduring symbol for the end of life.

FLEXIBLE HANDS
Each hand has 27 bones, and as many joints (p. 49). The human hand can be brought into almost any position relative to the body through rotation at the shoulder (p. 48) and movements of the forearm and wrist bones.

FORECASTING THE FUTURE
Tarot cards, the oldest playing cards in use today, are supposed to reveal the future - in this case, the future is very short.

XIII

LA MORT

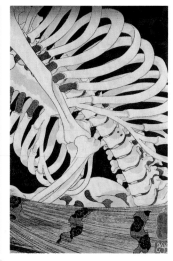

EASTERN MAGIC
Mitsukuni, a Japanese sorceress, summons up a giant skeleton to frighten her enemies in this painting by Kuniyoshi.

THE LONGEST BONES
The bones in the leg are the longest in the human body (p. 54). The leg bones are shaped in such a way as to allow their lower ends - at the ankles and knees - to touch, while the tops of the thigh bones - at the hip - may be more than 30 cm (1 ft) apart.

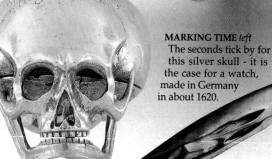

MARKING TIME *left*
The seconds tick by for this silver skull - it is the case for a watch, made in Germany in about 1620.

Detail of distorted skull shown in the painting on the right

ARTIST'S ILLUSION
Hans Holbein's *The Ambassadors* (1533) records the opulence of Henry VIII's court;

the odd shape in the foreground is a distorted skull, seen more clearly from one side and very close. (The name Holbein can be translated as "hollow bone".)

THE LOCKING KNEE
The knee is the largest joint in the body (p. 54), carrying as it does almost half the body's weight. It forms a locking hinge that bends in one direction only.

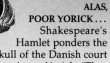

ALAS, POOR YORICK ...
Shakespeare's Hamlet ponders the skull of the Danish court jester Yorick: "That skull had a tongue in it, and could sing once ..."

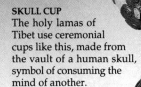

SKULL CUP
The holy lamas of Tibet use ceremonial cups like this, made from the vault of a human skull, symbol of consuming the mind of another.

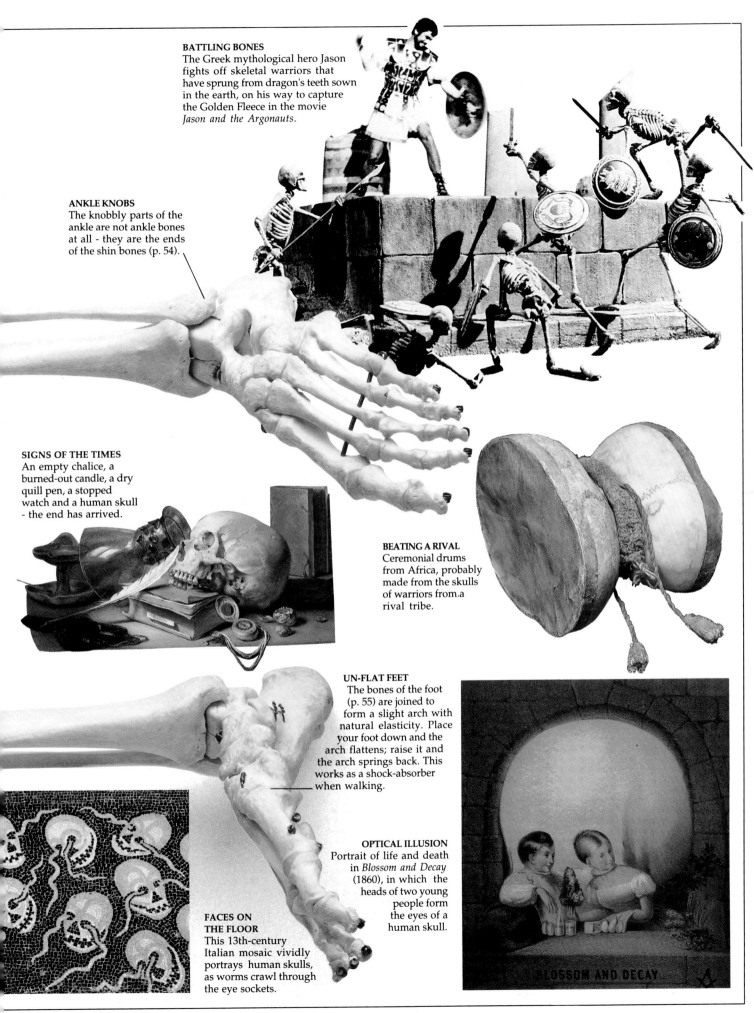

BATTLING BONES
The Greek mythological hero Jason fights off skeletal warriors that have sprung from dragon's teeth sown in the earth, on his way to capture the Golden Fleece in the movie *Jason and the Argonauts*.

ANKLE KNOBS
The knobbly parts of the ankle are not ankle bones at all - they are the ends of the shin bones (p. 54).

SIGNS OF THE TIMES
An empty chalice, a burned-out candle, a dry quill pen, a stopped watch and a human skull - the end has arrived.

BEATING A RIVAL
Ceremonial drums from Africa, probably made from the skulls of warriors from.a rival tribe.

UN-FLAT FEET
The bones of the foot (p. 55) are joined to form a slight arch with natural elasticity. Place your foot down and the arch flattens; raise it and the arch springs back. This works as a shock-absorber when walking.

OPTICAL ILLUSION
Portrait of life and death in *Blossom and Decay* (1860), in which the heads of two young people form the eyes of a human skull.

FACES ON THE FLOOR
This 13th-century Italian mosaic vividly portrays human skulls, as worms crawl through the eye sockets.

BLOSSOM AND DECAY

From bone to stone

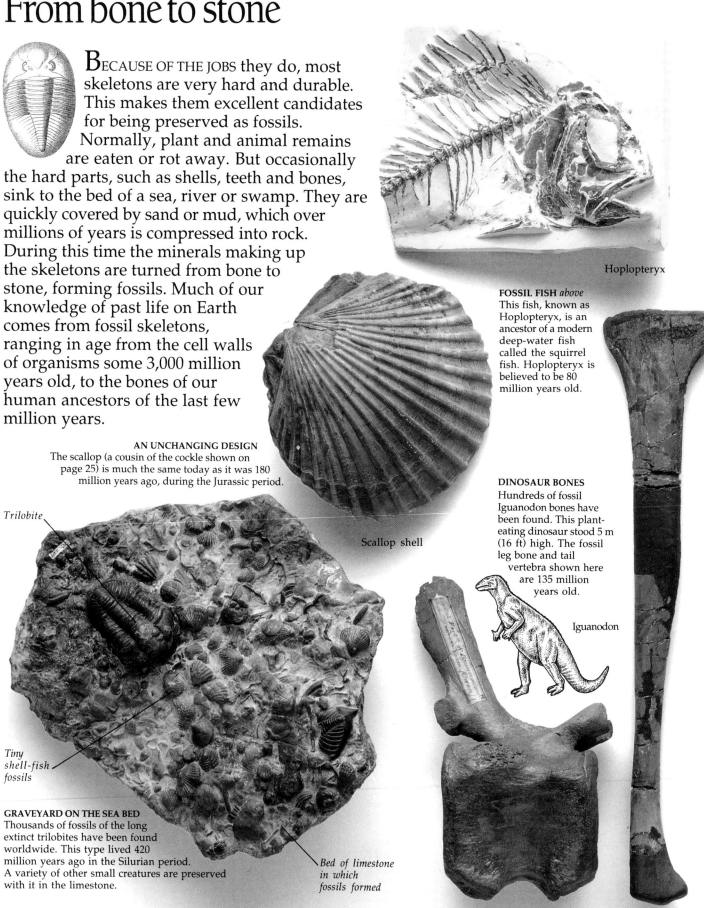

BECAUSE OF THE JOBS they do, most skeletons are very hard and durable. This makes them excellent candidates for being preserved as fossils. Normally, plant and animal remains are eaten or rot away. But occasionally the hard parts, such as shells, teeth and bones, sink to the bed of a sea, river or swamp. They are quickly covered by sand or mud, which over millions of years is compressed into rock. During this time the minerals making up the skeletons are turned from bone to stone, forming fossils. Much of our knowledge of past life on Earth comes from fossil skeletons, ranging in age from the cell walls of organisms some 3,000 million years old, to the bones of our human ancestors of the last few million years.

Hoplopteryx

FOSSIL FISH *above*
This fish, known as Hoplopteryx, is an ancestor of a modern deep-water fish called the squirrel fish. Hoplopteryx is believed to be 80 million years old.

AN UNCHANGING DESIGN
The scallop (a cousin of the cockle shown on page 25) is much the same today as it was 180 million years ago, during the Jurassic period.

Scallop shell

DINOSAUR BONES
Hundreds of fossil Iguanodon bones have been found. This plant-eating dinosaur stood 5 m (16 ft) high. The fossil leg bone and tail vertebra shown here are 135 million years old.

Iguanodon

Trilobite

Tiny shell-fish fossils

GRAVEYARD ON THE SEA BED
Thousands of fossils of the long extinct trilobites have been found worldwide. This type lived 420 million years ago in the Silurian period. A variety of other small creatures are preserved with it in the limestone.

Bed of limestone in which fossils formed

Single vertebra from the dinosaur's tail

Fibula or lower leg bone

Complete Ichthyosaur skeleton

Eyesocket

The conical teeth were all the same size

G 809

AN ANCIENT REPTILE *above*
The fish-eating Ichthyosaurs were marine reptiles shaped like modern-day dolphins. This skull, with its rows of conical teeth, comes from 180-million-year-old Jurassic rocks.

19th-century engraving of ammonite

Gas-filled whorls

Ammonite

Occupied whorl

Plesiosaur teeth (180 million years old)

Dagger-like shape for catching slippery fish

Shark's tooth (20 million years old)

Belemnite

LIVING IN A WHORL *above*
Ammonites were very common 180 million years ago. The octopus-like occupant lived in the large outer whorl; the other whorls were gas filled, for buoyancy. It was a relative of the nautilus (p. 25).

THE BELEMNITE'S BULLET *below*
Belemnites were related to squids and cuttlefish. They lived 340 to 50 million years ago. This bullet-shaped fossil, called a "guard", is the part of the body that protected the pointed end of the animal.

FISH-CATCHING TEETH *above*
The original owner of this shark's tooth was some 18 m (60 ft) long with a mouth gape of 2 m (6 ft). The smaller teeth are from a Plesiosaur - an extinct, long-necked sea reptile.

Guard from belemnite

SPINED FOR STABILITY *left*
This spiny scallop fossil (its smooth relative is opposite) is from Cretaceous rocks about 80 million years old. The spines provided the scallop with a grip on the slippery sea bed.

Tusks are upside-down on this skeleton

THE FOSSIL RECORD *right*
Fossil skeletons, like this one of a giant mammoth, are often the only evidence we have of animals now long extinct.

Spiny scallop shell

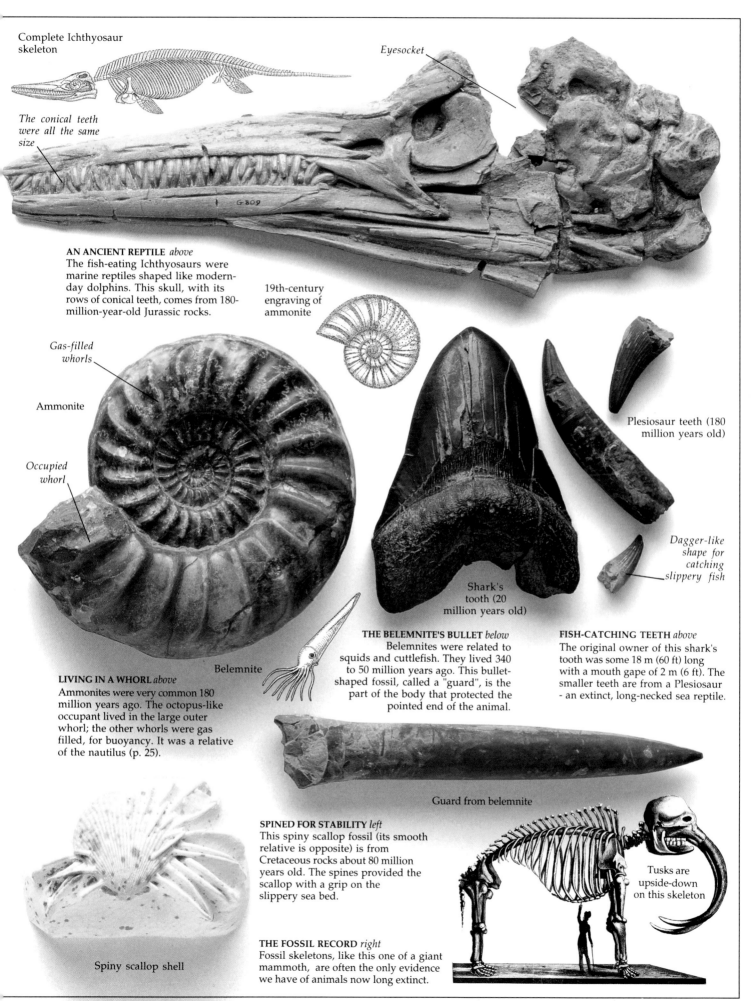

Mammals

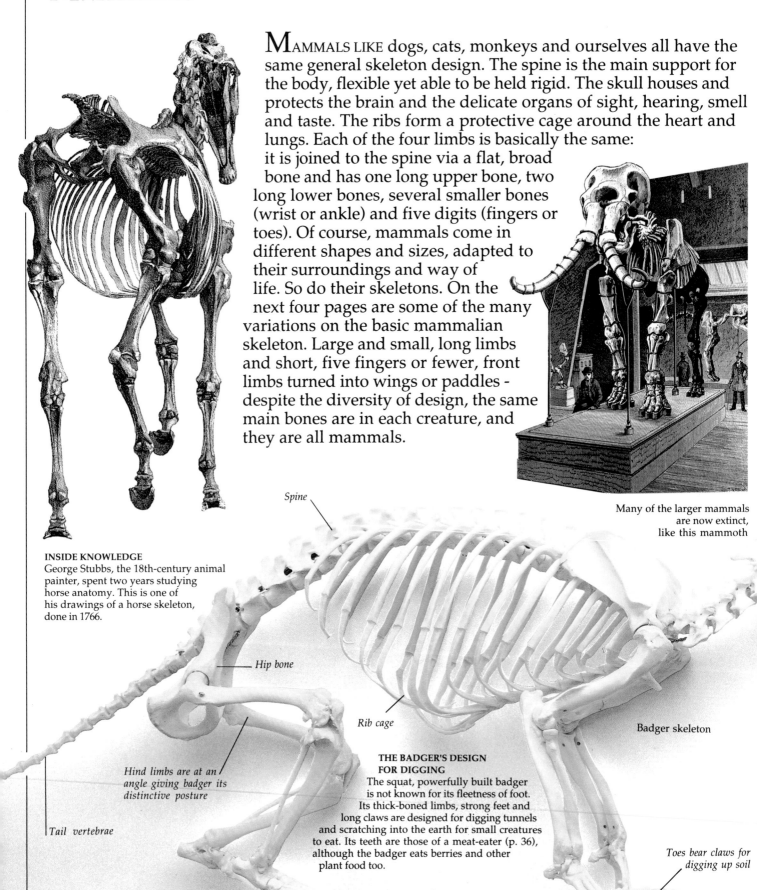

MAMMALS LIKE dogs, cats, monkeys and ourselves all have the same general skeleton design. The spine is the main support for the body, flexible yet able to be held rigid. The skull houses and protects the brain and the delicate organs of sight, hearing, smell and taste. The ribs form a protective cage around the heart and lungs. Each of the four limbs is basically the same: it is joined to the spine via a flat, broad bone and has one long upper bone, two long lower bones, several smaller bones (wrist or ankle) and five digits (fingers or toes). Of course, mammals come in different shapes and sizes, adapted to their surroundings and way of life. So do their skeletons. On the next four pages are some of the many variations on the basic mammalian skeleton. Large and small, long limbs and short, five fingers or fewer, front limbs turned into wings or paddles - despite the diversity of design, the same main bones are in each creature, and they are all mammals.

Many of the larger mammals are now extinct, like this mammoth

INSIDE KNOWLEDGE
George Stubbs, the 18th-century animal painter, spent two years studying horse anatomy. This is one of his drawings of a horse skeleton, done in 1766.

Spine

Hip bone

Rib cage

Badger skeleton

THE BADGER'S DESIGN FOR DIGGING
The squat, powerfully built badger is not known for its fleetness of foot. Its thick-boned limbs, strong feet and long claws are designed for digging tunnels and scratching into the earth for small creatures to eat. Its teeth are those of a meat-eater (p. 36), although the badger eats berries and other plant food too.

Hind limbs are at an angle giving badger its distinctive posture

Tail vertebrae

Toes bear claws for digging up soil

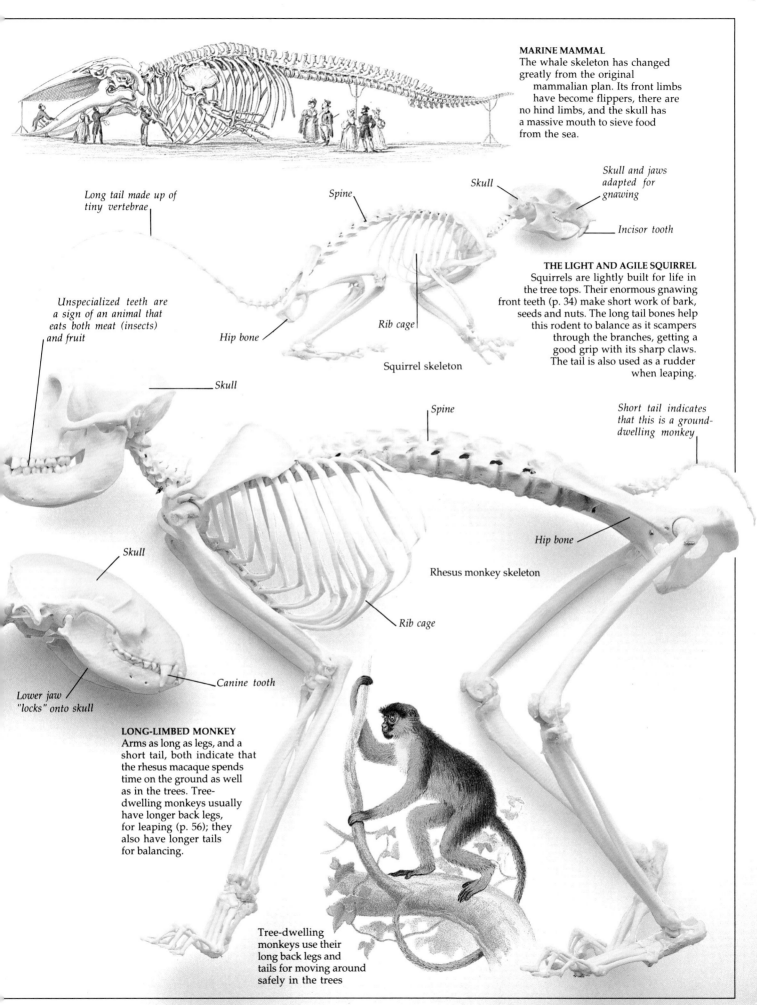

MARINE MAMMAL
The whale skeleton has changed greatly from the original mammalian plan. Its front limbs have become flippers, there are no hind limbs, and the skull has a massive mouth to sieve food from the sea.

Long tail made up of tiny vertebrae

Spine

Skull

Skull and jaws adapted for gnawing

Incisor tooth

THE LIGHT AND AGILE SQUIRREL
Squirrels are lightly built for life in the tree tops. Their enormous gnawing front teeth (p. 34) make short work of bark, seeds and nuts. The long tail bones help this rodent to balance as it scampers through the branches, getting a good grip with its sharp claws. The tail is also used as a rudder when leaping.

Unspecialized teeth are a sign of an animal that eats both meat (insects) and fruit

Hip bone

Rib cage

Squirrel skeleton

Skull

Spine

Short tail indicates that this is a ground-dwelling monkey

Hip bone

Rhesus monkey skeleton

Skull

Rib cage

Canine tooth

Lower jaw "locks" onto skull

LONG-LIMBED MONKEY
Arms as long as legs, and a short tail, both indicate that the rhesus macaque spends time on the ground as well as in the trees. Tree-dwelling monkeys usually have longer back legs, for leaping (p. 56); they also have longer tails for balancing.

Tree-dwelling monkeys use their long back legs and tails for moving around safely in the trees

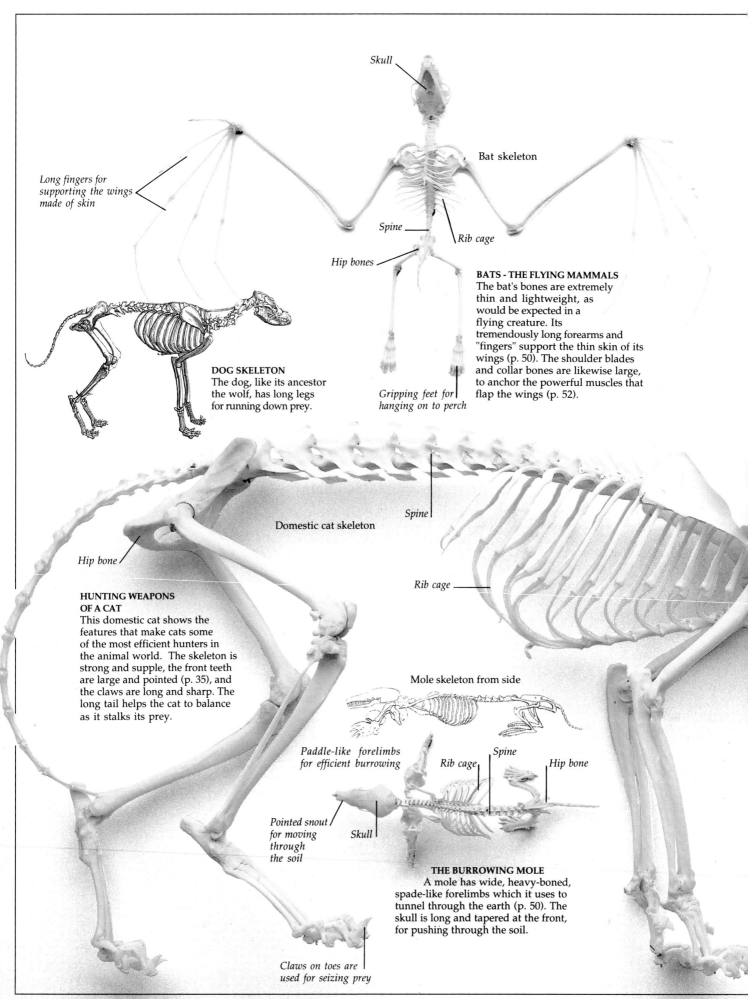

Skull

Bat skeleton

*Long fingers for
supporting the wings
made of skin*

Spine

Rib cage

Hip bones

BATS - THE FLYING MAMMALS
The bat's bones are extremely
thin and lightweight, as
would be expected in a
flying creature. Its
tremendously long forearms and
"fingers" support the thin skin of its
wings (p. 50). The shoulder blades
and collar bones are likewise large,
to anchor the powerful muscles that
flap the wings (p. 52).

*Gripping feet for
hanging on to perch*

DOG SKELETON
The dog, like its ancestor
the wolf, has long legs
for running down prey.

Domestic cat skeleton

Spine

Hip bone

Rib cage

HUNTING WEAPONS
OF A CAT
This domestic cat shows the
features that make cats some
of the most efficient hunters in
the animal world. The skeleton is
strong and supple, the front teeth
are large and pointed (p. 35), and
the claws are long and sharp. The
long tail helps the cat to balance
as it stalks its prey.

Mole skeleton from side

*Paddle-like forelimbs
for efficient burrowing*

Spine

Rib cage

Hip bone

*Pointed snout
for moving
through
the soil*

Skull

THE BURROWING MOLE
A mole has wide, heavy-boned,
spade-like forelimbs which it uses to
tunnel through the earth (p. 50). The
skull is long and tapered at the front,
for pushing through the soil.

*Claws on toes are
used for seizing prey*

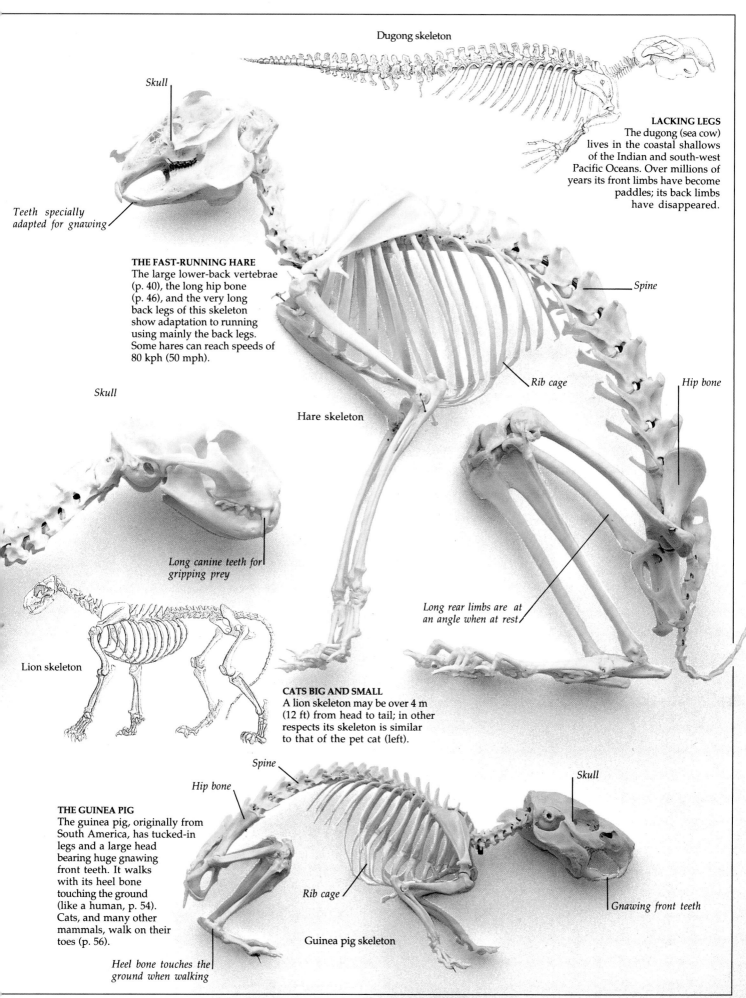

Dugong skeleton

Skull

Teeth specially adapted for gnawing

LACKING LEGS
The dugong (sea cow) lives in the coastal shallows of the Indian and south-west Pacific Oceans. Over millions of years its front limbs have become paddles; its back limbs have disappeared.

Spine

THE FAST-RUNNING HARE
The large lower-back vertebrae (p. 40), the long hip bone (p. 46), and the very long back legs of this skeleton show adaptation to running using mainly the back legs. Some hares can reach speeds of 80 kph (50 mph).

Rib cage

Hip bone

Skull

Hare skeleton

Long canine teeth for gripping prey

Long rear limbs are at an angle when at rest

Lion skeleton

CATS BIG AND SMALL
A lion skeleton may be over 4 m (12 ft) from head to tail; in other respects its skeleton is similar to that of the pet cat (left).

Spine

Skull

Hip bone

THE GUINEA PIG
The guinea pig, originally from South America, has tucked-in legs and a large head bearing huge gnawing front teeth. It walks with its heel bone touching the ground (like a human, p. 54). Cats, and many other mammals, walk on their toes (p. 56).

Rib cage

Gnawing front teeth

Guinea pig skeleton

Heel bone touches the ground when walking

Birds

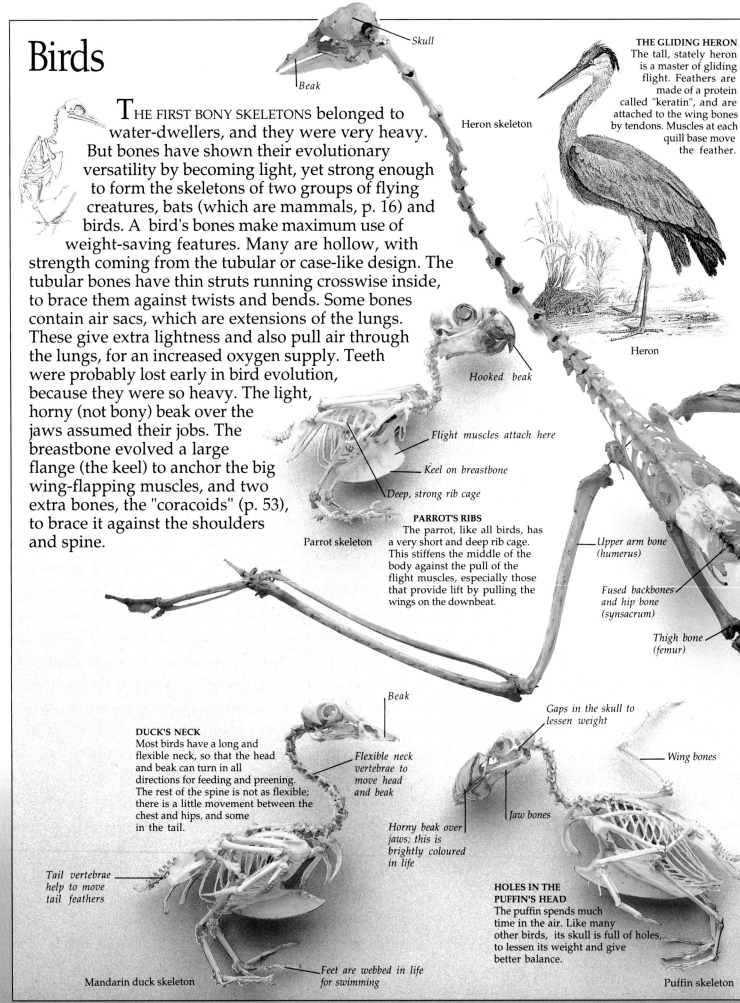

THE FIRST BONY SKELETONS belonged to water-dwellers, and they were very heavy. But bones have shown their evolutionary versatility by becoming light, yet strong enough to form the skeletons of two groups of flying creatures, bats (which are mammals, p. 16) and birds. A bird's bones make maximum use of weight-saving features. Many are hollow, with strength coming from the tubular or case-like design. The tubular bones have thin struts running crosswise inside, to brace them against twists and bends. Some bones contain air sacs, which are extensions of the lungs. These give extra lightness and also pull air through the lungs, for an increased oxygen supply. Teeth were probably lost early in bird evolution, because they were so heavy. The light, horny (not bony) beak over the jaws assumed their jobs. The breastbone evolved a large flange (the keel) to anchor the big wing-flapping muscles, and two extra bones, the "coracoids" (p. 53), to brace it against the shoulders and spine.

Skull

Beak

Heron skeleton

THE GLIDING HERON
The tall, stately heron is a master of gliding flight. Feathers are made of a protein called "keratin", and are attached to the wing bones by tendons. Muscles at each quill base move the feather.

Heron

Hooked beak

Flight muscles attach here

Keel on breastbone

Deep, strong rib cage

Parrot skeleton

PARROT'S RIBS
The parrot, like all birds, has a very short and deep rib cage. This stiffens the middle of the body against the pull of the flight muscles, especially those that provide lift by pulling the wings on the downbeat.

Upper arm bone (humerus)

Fused backbones and hip bone (synsacrum)

Thigh bone (femur)

Beak

DUCK'S NECK
Most birds have a long and flexible neck, so that the head and beak can turn in all directions for feeding and preening. The rest of the spine is not as flexible; there is a little movement between the chest and hips, and some in the tail.

Flexible neck vertebrae to move head and beak

Gaps in the skull to lessen weight

Wing bones

Jaw bones

Horny beak over jaws; this is brightly coloured in life

Tail vertebrae help to move tail feathers

HOLES IN THE PUFFIN'S HEAD
The puffin spends much time in the air. Like many other birds, its skull is full of holes, to lessen its weight and give better balance.

Feet are webbed in life for swimming

Mandarin duck skeleton

Puffin skeleton

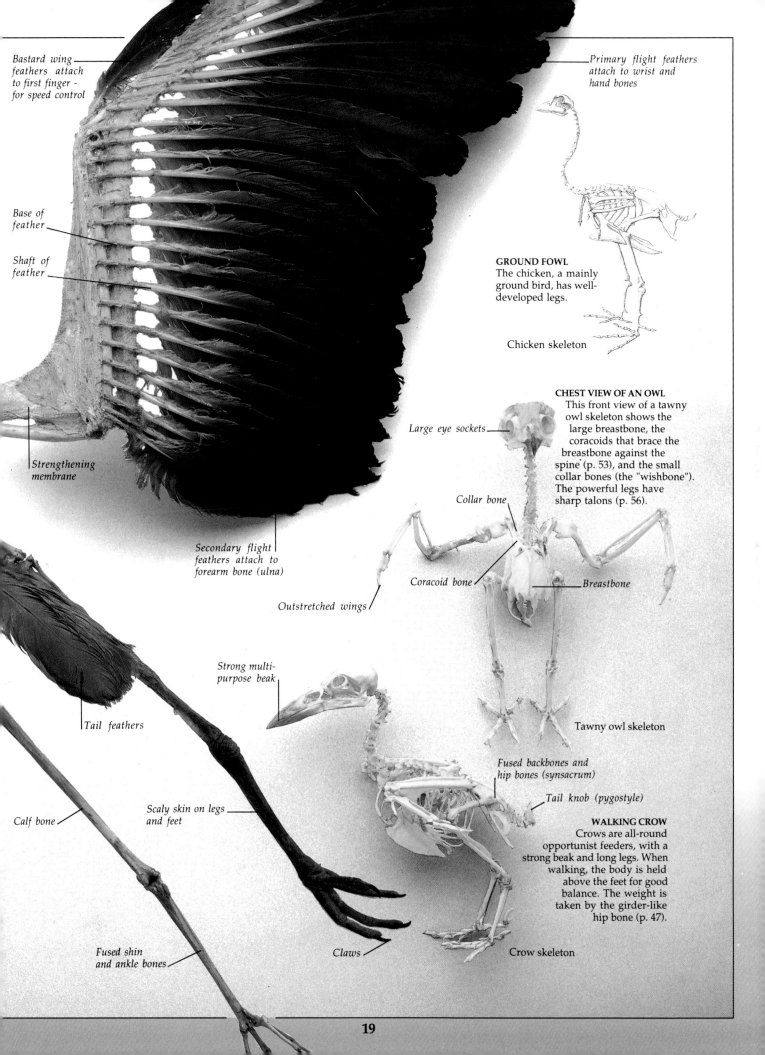

Bastard wing feathers attach to first finger - for speed control

Base of feather

Shaft of feather

Strengthening membrane

Primary flight feathers attach to wrist and hand bones

GROUND FOWL
The chicken, a mainly ground bird, has well-developed legs.

Chicken skeleton

CHEST VIEW OF AN OWL
This front view of a tawny owl skeleton shows the large breastbone, the coracoids that brace the breastbone against the spine (p. 53), and the small collar bones (the "wishbone"). The powerful legs have sharp talons (p. 56).

Large eye sockets

Collar bone

Coracoid bone

Breastbone

Secondary flight feathers attach to forearm bone (ulna)

Outstretched wings

Tawny owl skeleton

Fused backbones and hip bones (synsacrum)

Tail knob (pygostyle)

Strong multi-purpose beak

Tail feathers

Calf bone

Scaly skin on legs and feet

Fused shin and ankle bones

Claws

WALKING CROW
Crows are all-round opportunist feeders, with a strong beak and long legs. When walking, the body is held above the feet for good balance. The weight is taken by the girder-like hip bone (p. 47).

Crow skeleton

Fish, reptiles and amphibians

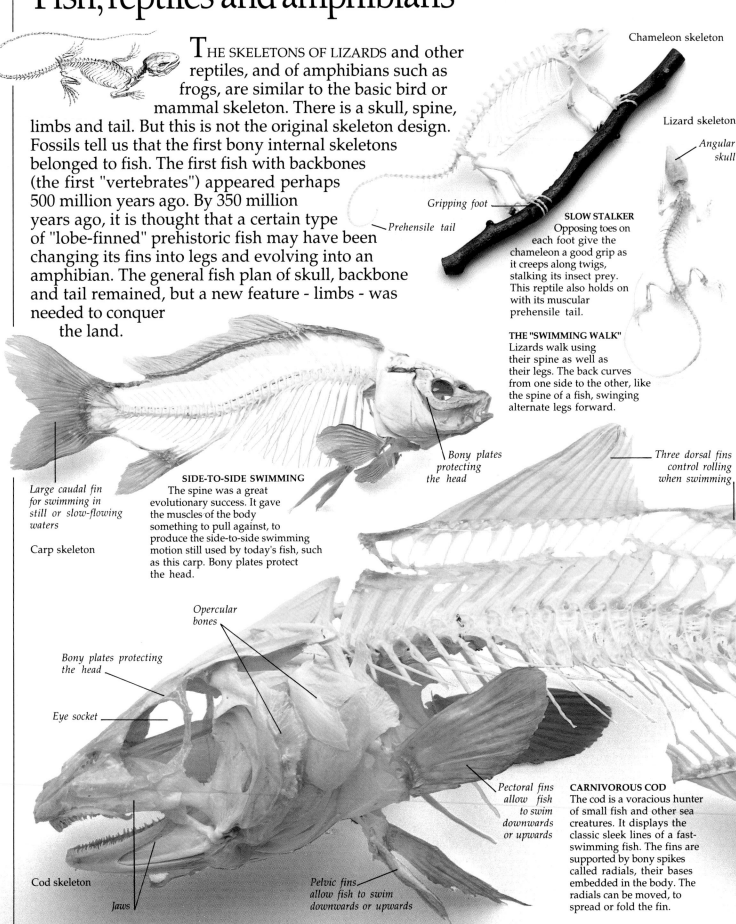

THE SKELETONS OF LIZARDS and other reptiles, and of amphibians such as frogs, are similar to the basic bird or mammal skeleton. There is a skull, spine, limbs and tail. But this is not the original skeleton design. Fossils tell us that the first bony internal skeletons belonged to fish. The first fish with backbones (the first "vertebrates") appeared perhaps 500 million years ago. By 350 million years ago, it is thought that a certain type of "lobe-finned" prehistoric fish may have been changing its fins into legs and evolving into an amphibian. The general fish plan of skull, backbone and tail remained, but a new feature - limbs - was needed to conquer the land.

Chameleon skeleton

Lizard skeleton

Angular skull

Gripping foot

Prehensile tail

SLOW STALKER
Opposing toes on each foot give the chameleon a good grip as it creeps along twigs, stalking its insect prey. This reptile also holds on with its muscular prehensile tail.

THE "SWIMMING WALK"
Lizards walk using their spine as well as their legs. The back curves from one side to the other, like the spine of a fish, swinging alternate legs forward.

Bony plates protecting the head

SIDE-TO-SIDE SWIMMING
The spine was a great evolutionary success. It gave the muscles of the body something to pull against, to produce the side-to-side swimming motion still used by today's fish, such as this carp. Bony plates protect the head.

Large caudal fin for swimming in still or slow-flowing waters

Carp skeleton

Three dorsal fins control rolling when swimming

Opercular bones

Bony plates protecting the head

Eye socket

Pectoral fins allow fish to swim downwards or upwards

CARNIVOROUS COD
The cod is a voracious hunter of small fish and other sea creatures. It displays the classic sleek lines of a fast-swimming fish. The fins are supported by bony spikes called radials, their bases embedded in the body. The radials can be moved, to spread or fold the fin.

Cod skeleton

Jaws

Pelvic fins allow fish to swim downwards or upwards

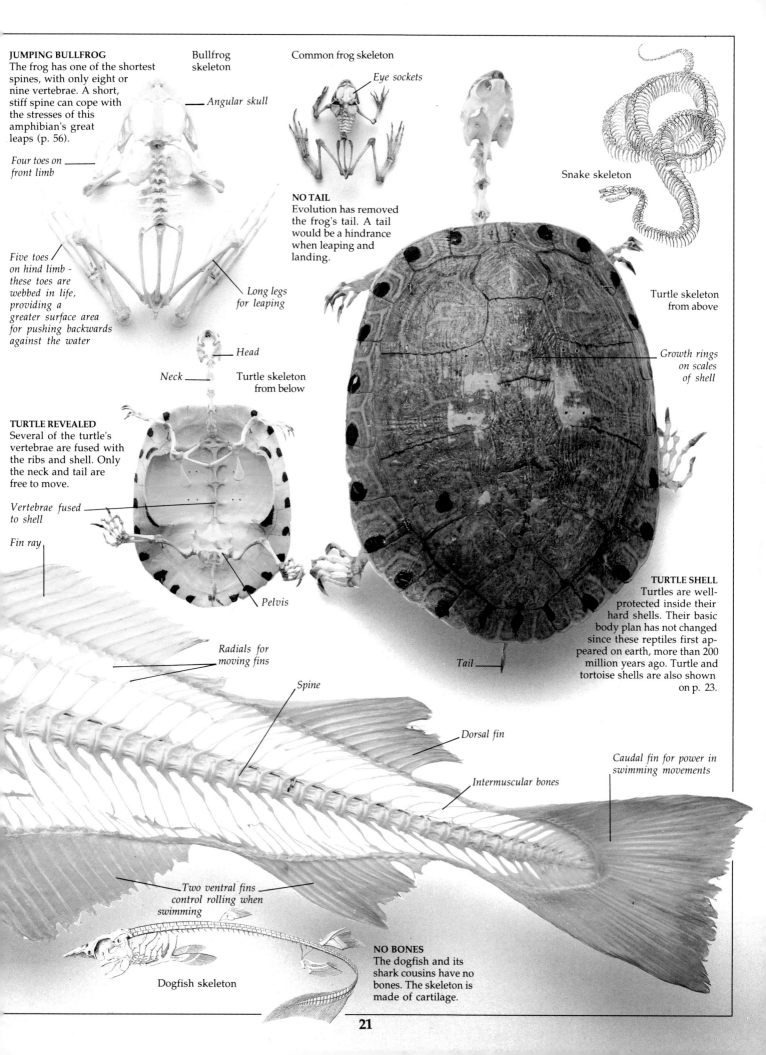

JUMPING BULLFROG
The frog has one of the shortest spines, with only eight or nine vertebrae. A short, stiff spine can cope with the stresses of this amphibian's great leaps (p. 56).

Four toes on front limb

Five toes on hind limb - these toes are webbed in life, providing a greater surface area for pushing backwards against the water

Bullfrog skeleton

Angular skull

Common frog skeleton

Eye sockets

NO TAIL
Evolution has removed the frog's tail. A tail would be a hindrance when leaping and landing.

Long legs for leaping

Snake skeleton

Turtle skeleton from above

Growth rings on scales of shell

Head

Neck

Turtle skeleton from below

TURTLE REVEALED
Several of the turtle's vertebrae are fused with the ribs and shell. Only the neck and tail are free to move.

Vertebrae fused to shell

Fin ray

Pelvis

TURTLE SHELL
Turtles are well-protected inside their hard shells. Their basic body plan has not changed since these reptiles first appeared on earth, more than 200 million years ago. Turtle and tortoise shells are also shown on p. 23.

Tail

Radials for moving fins

Spine

Dorsal fin

Intermuscular bones

Caudal fin for power in swimming movements

Two ventral fins control rolling when swimming

Dogfish skeleton

NO BONES
The dogfish and its shark cousins have no bones. The skeleton is made of cartilage.

Skeletons on the outside

THE VAST MAJORITY of animals do not have a bony internal skeleton. Insects, spiders, shellfish and other invertebrates have a hard outer casing called an "exoskeleton". This exoskeleton does the same job as an internal skeleton, providing strength and support. It also forms a hard, protective shield around the soft inner organs. But it does have drawbacks. It cannot expand, so the animal must grow by moulting its old exoskeleton and making a new, larger one. Above a certain size it becomes so thick and heavy that the muscles cannot move it. This is why animals with exoskeletons tend to be small.

Magnification X40

MICROSKELETONS
Diatoms float in their billions in the oceans. These single-celled organisms trap the sun's light energy to grow, like plants. They construct silica casings around themselves, presumably for protection. These "skeletons" are amazingly elaborate and beautiful in shape and variety.

WOOD-BORING BEETLE
This metallic purple and yellow beetle has a larva that bores under the bark of trees.

WOOD-BORING BEETLE
Larvae of this wood borer can live up to 30 years.

WOOD-BORING BEETLE
The larva of this brilliant green beetle can be a serious timber pest.

LEAF BEETLE
A brilliant green exoskeleton camouflages the beetle among leaves.

FEMALE RHINOCEROS BEETLE
This beetle makes a dung-filled burrow as food for its young.

STAG BEETLE
The male's jaws cannot bite hard - their muscles are too weak.

DARKLING BEETLE
Long antennae help this beetle feel its way around.

ALL-OVER ARMOUR
Like other insects, beetles are well protected by a tough exoskeleton made of a hard, waterproof material called chitin. The wing cases were once another pair of wings, since modified by evolution. This goliath beetle is the heaviest insect, weighing 100 g (3·5 oz).

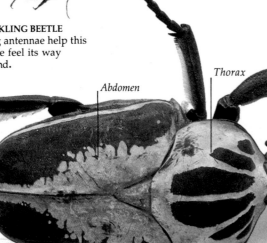

Abdomen

Thorax

Head

Eye

Jointed limb

Goliath beetle

Wing case

Leg muscles are inside tubular leg skeleton

Transparent wing

THE WINGS REVEALED
Under the hard outer wing cases lie the delicate, transparent wings used for flight. The long legs have many joints.

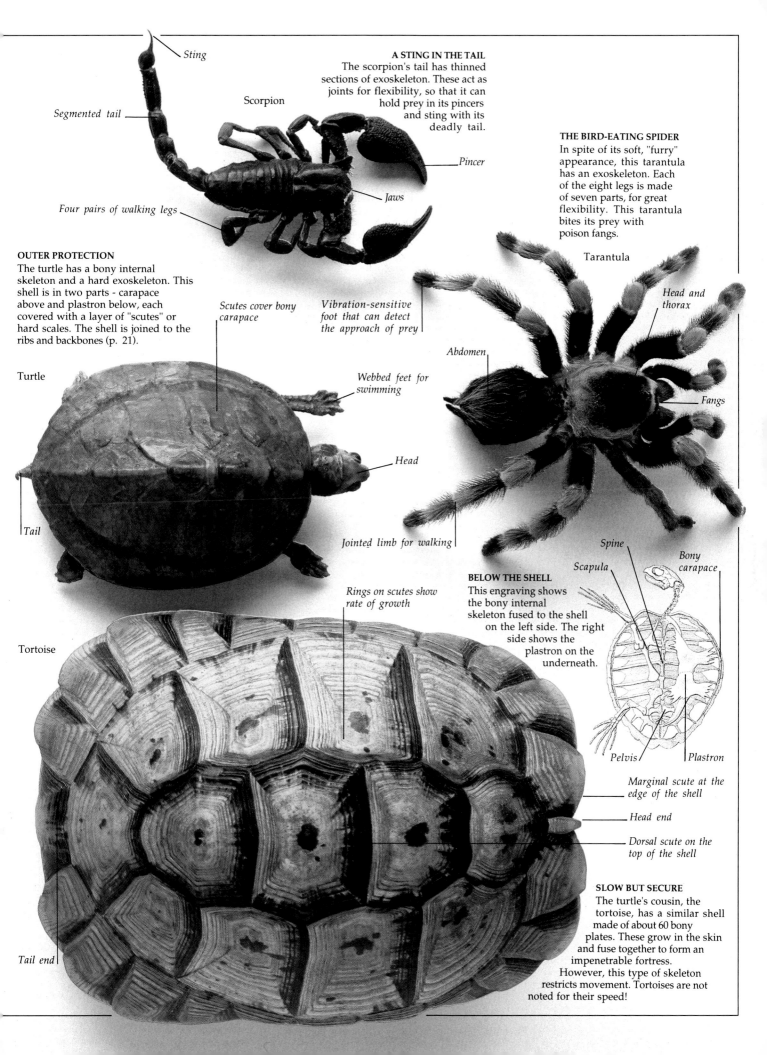

Sting

Segmented tail

Scorpion

Four pairs of walking legs

A STING IN THE TAIL
The scorpion's tail has thinned
sections of exoskeleton. These act as
joints for flexibility, so that it can
hold prey in its pincers
and sting with its
deadly tail.

Pincer

Jaws

THE BIRD-EATING SPIDER
In spite of its soft, "furry"
appearance, this tarantula
has an exoskeleton. Each
of the eight legs is made
of seven parts, for great
flexibility. This tarantula
bites its prey with
poison fangs.

Tarantula

_Head and
thorax_

OUTER PROTECTION
The turtle has a bony internal
skeleton and a hard exoskeleton. This
shell is in two parts - carapace
above and plastron below, each
covered with a layer of "scutes" or
hard scales. The shell is joined to the
ribs and backbones (p. 21).

_Scutes cover bony
carapace_

_Vibration-sensitive
foot that can detect
the approach of prey_

Abdomen

Fangs

Turtle

_Webbed feet for
swimming_

Head

Tail

Jointed limb for walking

Spine

Scapula

_Bony
carapace_

_Rings on scutes show
rate of growth_

BELOW THE SHELL
This engraving shows
the bony internal
skeleton fused to the shell
on the left side. The right
side shows the
plastron on the
underneath.

Tortoise

Pelvis

Plastron

_Marginal scute at the
edge of the shell_

Head end

_Dorsal scute on the
top of the shell_

SLOW BUT SECURE
The turtle's cousin, the
tortoise, has a similar shell
made of about 60 bony
plates. These grow in the skin
and fuse together to form an
impenetrable fortress.
However, this type of skeleton
restricts movement. Tortoises are not
noted for their speed!

Tail end

Marine exoskeletons

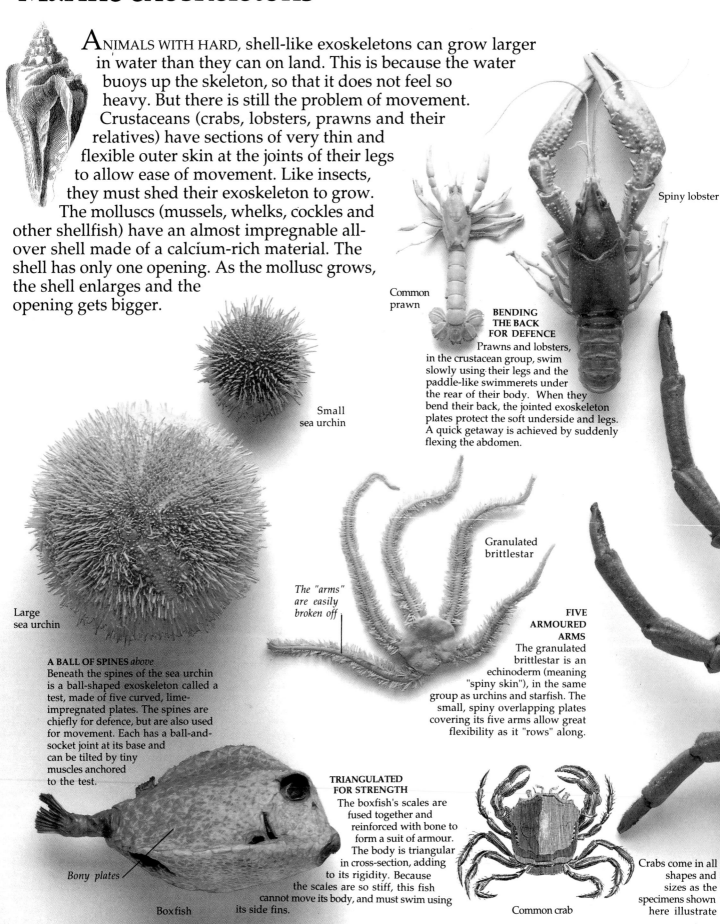

ANIMALS WITH HARD, shell-like exoskeletons can grow larger in water than they can on land. This is because the water buoys up the skeleton, so that it does not feel so heavy. But there is still the problem of movement. Crustaceans (crabs, lobsters, prawns and their relatives) have sections of very thin and flexible outer skin at the joints of their legs to allow ease of movement. Like insects, they must shed their exoskeleton to grow. The molluscs (mussels, whelks, cockles and other shellfish) have an almost impregnable all-over shell made of a calcium-rich material. The shell has only one opening. As the mollusc grows, the shell enlarges and the opening gets bigger.

Spiny lobster

Common prawn

Small sea urchin

BENDING THE BACK FOR DEFENCE
Prawns and lobsters, in the crustacean group, swim slowly using their legs and the paddle-like swimmerets under the rear of their body. When they bend their back, the jointed exoskeleton plates protect the soft underside and legs. A quick getaway is achieved by suddenly flexing the abdomen.

Granulated brittlestar

Large sea urchin

The "arms" are easily broken off

FIVE ARMOURED ARMS
The granulated brittlestar is an echinoderm (meaning "spiny skin"), in the same group as urchins and starfish. The small, spiny overlapping plates covering its five arms allow great flexibility as it "rows" along.

A BALL OF SPINES *above*
Beneath the spines of the sea urchin is a ball-shaped exoskeleton called a test, made of five curved, lime-impregnated plates. The spines are chiefly for defence, but are also used for movement. Each has a ball-and-socket joint at its base and can be tilted by tiny muscles anchored to the test.

TRIANGULATED FOR STRENGTH
The boxfish's scales are fused together and reinforced with bone to form a suit of armour. The body is triangular in cross-section, adding to its rigidity. Because the scales are so stiff, this fish cannot move its body, and must swim using its side fins.

Bony plates

Boxfish

Common crab

Crabs come in all shapes and sizes as the specimens shown here illustrate

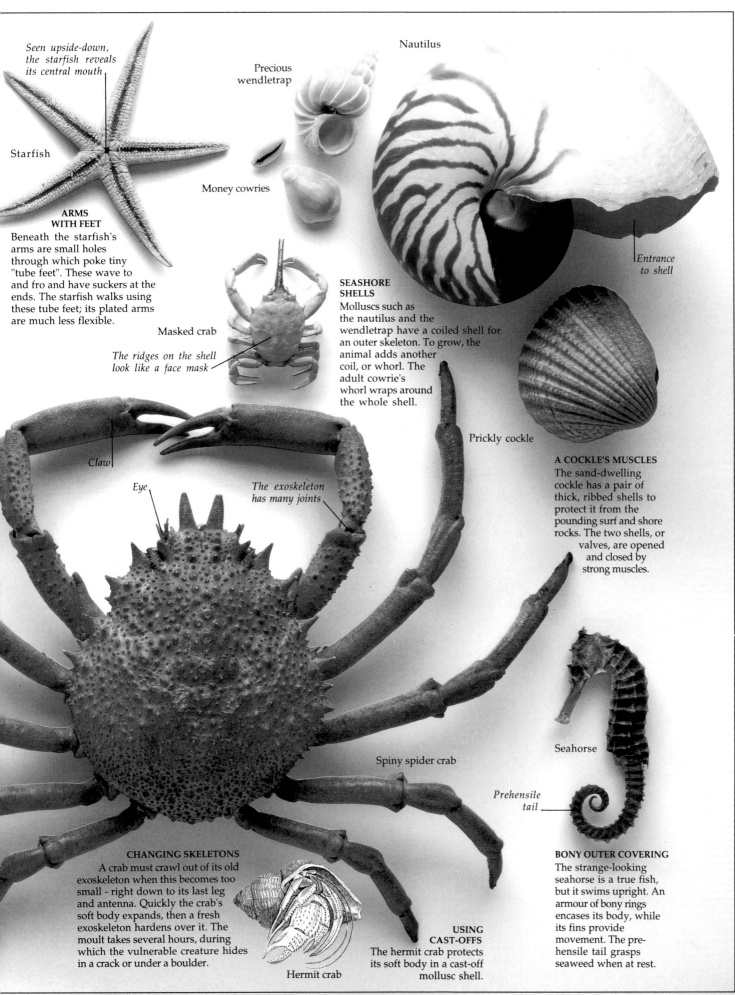

Seen upside-down, the starfish reveals its central mouth

Nautilus

Precious wendletrap

Starfish

Money cowries

Entrance to shell

ARMS WITH FEET

Beneath the starfish's arms are small holes through which poke tiny "tube feet". These wave to and fro and have suckers at the ends. The starfish walks using these tube feet; its plated arms are much less flexible.

Masked crab

SEASHORE SHELLS

Molluscs such as the nautilus and the wendletrap have a coiled shell for an outer skeleton. To grow, the animal adds another coil, or whorl. The adult cowrie's whorl wraps around the whole shell.

The ridges on the shell look like a face mask

Prickly cockle

A COCKLE'S MUSCLES

The sand-dwelling cockle has a pair of thick, ribbed shells to protect it from the pounding surf and shore rocks. The two shells, or valves, are opened and closed by strong muscles.

Claw

Eye

The exoskeleton has many joints

Spiny spider crab

Seahorse

Prehensile tail

CHANGING SKELETONS

A crab must crawl out of its old exoskeleton when this becomes too small - right down to its last leg and antenna. Quickly the crab's soft body expands, then a fresh exoskeleton hardens over it. The moult takes several hours, during which the vulnerable creature hides in a crack or under a boulder.

Hermit crab

USING CAST-OFFS

The hermit crab protects its soft body in a cast-off mollusc shell.

BONY OUTER COVERING

The strange-looking seahorse is a true fish, but it swims upright. An armour of bony rings encases its body, while its fins provide movement. The prehensile tail grasps seaweed when at rest.

25

The human skull and teeth

ALTHOUGH THE HEAD is at one end of the human body, it functions as the body's centre. The skull protects the brain, which is the central coordinator for receiving information from the outside world and organizing the body's reactions. The special senses of sight, hearing, smell and taste are concentrated in the skull. In particular, the eyes and inner ears (where the delicate organs of hearing are sited) lie well protected in bony recesses. Air, containing the oxygen vital to life, passes into the body through the skull. So does food, being crushed first by the jaws and teeth so that it can be swallowed and digested more easily. The senses of smell and taste are well positioned to check air and food for noxious odours and flavours.

THIS WON'T HURT . . .
Teeth are both tough and sensitive. A visit to a medieval dentist was a painful affair, although it would hopefully give merciful relief from long-term nagging toothache.

BRAINBOX
The delicate, blancmange-like brain tissue is surrounded by a bony box. Its internal volume is some 1,500 cc (about 2.5 pints).

A COLOURED SKULL
A computer-coloured X-ray shows the bones in the skull and neck. The soft tissues of the nose, which is not made of bone, also show up.

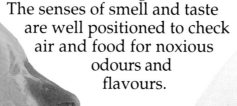

Incisor tooth
Canine tooth
Premolar tooth
Molar tooth
Roof of mouth
Nasal passages and sinuses
Lower jaw fits here
Outer ear canal
Hole for carotid artery
Uppermost vertebra fits here
Hole for spinal cord

THE BASE OF THE SKULL
This unfamiliar underview of the skull, with the lower jaw removed, shows the delicate internal partitioning. (The individual bones of the skull are identified on pp. 28-9.)

EYE HOLE
The eye socket, or orbit, protects the eyeball, which is a sphere about 25 mm (1 in) across. The socket is larger; sandwiched between the eyeball and the socket are cushioning pads of fat, nerves and blood vessels, and the muscles that move the eye.

NERVE HOLE
Many nerves lead to and from the brain through holes in the skull. This hole, the "infra-orbital foramen", is for nerve branches from the upper incisor, canine and premolar teeth.

TOOTH HOLES
The bone of the jaw is spongy in texture and anchors the roots of the teeth.

NOSE HOLE
The protruding hump of the human nose is made of cartilage, not bone, so it is absent from the skeleton of the skull.

The teeth

An adult human has 32 teeth. In each jaw (upper and lower) there are four incisors at the front, then, on each side, one canine, and two premolars plus three molars. The enamel of a tooth is the hardest substance in the body.

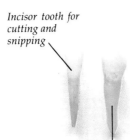

Incisor tooth for cutting and snipping

Canine tooth for piercing and tearing

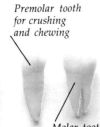

Premolar tooth for crushing and chewing

Molar tooth for crushing and chewing

INSIDE A TOOTH *right*
If a tooth is sliced open, various layers can be distinguished inside. The outer layer is enamel, a hard, protective substance. Under this is a tough layer of dentine, which surrounds the pulp, containing nerves and blood vessels.

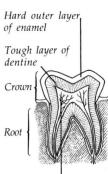

Hard outer layer of enamel

Tough layer of dentine

Crown

Root

Nerves and blood vessels of pulp

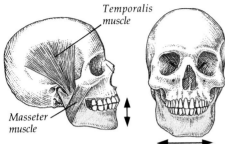

Temporalis muscle

Masseter muscle

ALL-ROUND CHEWING *above*
As we eat, the lower jaw moves up and down, and also from side to side, and even from front to back, for a really thorough chewing job. The tongue (which is almost all muscle) moves the food around the mouth, while the cheek muscles keep it pressed between the teeth.

GROWING TEETH *right*
A young child has a set of 20 milk (deciduous) teeth. Fewer teeth can fit in the smaller jaws. They fall out from the age of about six years, starting with those at the front.

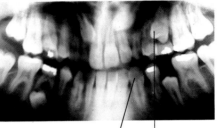

"Wrap-around" X-ray of child's teeth

Milk tooth

Permanent tooth developing in gum

BRAIN DOME
The human forehead is more dome-shaped and bulging than that of our ape relatives. It houses the cerebral cortex - the part of the brain associated with intelligence.

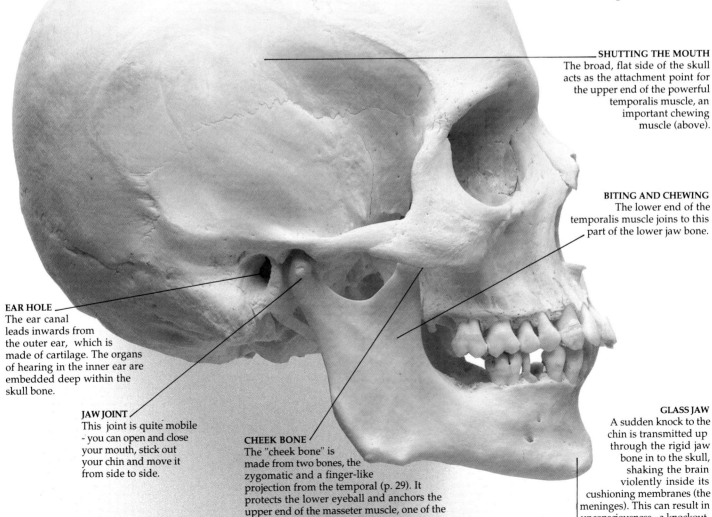

SHUTTING THE MOUTH
The broad, flat side of the skull acts as the attachment point for the upper end of the powerful temporalis muscle, an important chewing muscle (above).

BITING AND CHEWING
The lower end of the temporalis muscle joins to this part of the lower jaw bone.

EAR HOLE
The ear canal leads inwards from the outer ear, which is made of cartilage. The organs of hearing in the inner ear are embedded deep within the skull bone.

JAW JOINT
This joint is quite mobile - you can open and close your mouth, stick out your chin and move it from side to side.

CHEEK BONE
The "cheek bone" is made from two bones, the zygomatic and a finger-like projection from the temporal (p. 29). It protects the lower eyeball and anchors the upper end of the masseter muscle, one of the main chewing muscles (above).

GLASS JAW
A sudden knock to the chin is transmitted up through the rigid jaw bone in to the skull, shaking the brain violently inside its cushioning membranes (the meninges). This can result in unconsciousness - a knockout.

How the skull is built

THE HUMAN SKULL STARTS LIFE as an intricate curved jigsaw of nearly 30 separate pieces, sculpted in cartilage and membrane. During development these gradually turn to bone and grow together to form a solid case that protects the brain, eyes, inner ears, and other delicate sense organs. The separate bones are eventually knitted together with fibrous tissue. These joins, or "sutures", can be seen as wiggly lines on the skull. From the age of about 30 to 40 years, the sutures slowly fade and disappear. This is one way of telling the age of a skull's original owner. The cranium, or "brainbox", is made up of eight bones. There are 14 in the face, two each side of the upper jaw, and one in each side of the lower jaw. The skull also encases the smallest bones in the body – the six tiny ossicles of the inner ears – three on each side of the skull (p.59).

A SKELETON PONDERS A SKULL
This engraving by Vesalius, the founding father of anatomy, is thought to have been Shakespeare's inspiration for the graveyard scene in *Hamlet*.

Two maxillae bear the top teeth and form the roof of the mouth

Inferior concha warms and moistens air as it enters the nose

The palatine bone makes up the back of the roof of the mouth

The lower back of the nasal cavity is called the vomer

The mandible, or lower jaw, consists of two firmly joined halves

The nasal bones make up the bridge of the nose

Inferior concha

Palatine bone

Maxilla

The fontanelles

During birth, the baby's head is squeezed as it passes along the birth canal (p. 45). Fontanelles are "soft spots" in the baby's skull, where the membrane has not yet turned to bone. They allow the skull bones to mould, slide and even overlap, to minimize damage to the skull and brain. The largest of the six fontanelles is on the top of the skull. They disappear by one year of age.

Suture lines

The pulsing of the baby's blood system can often be seen beneath the thin membrane layer of the uppermost fontanelle.

Adult skull

Baby's skull

The flattening face

Fossils found so far give us a broad outline of how the human skull may have evolved. Some of our probable ancestors are shown on the right. Gradually the face has become flatter, the teeth smaller, the chin less protruding, and the forehead more domed, to house the increasingly large brain.

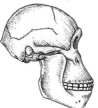

Australopithecus "Southern ape"

3-2 million years ago

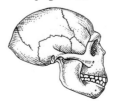

Homo erectus "Upright man"

750,000 years ago

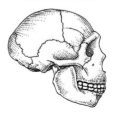

Homo sapiens neanderthalensis "Neanderthal man"

100,000-40,000 years ago

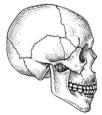

Homo sapiens sapiens "Wise man"

40,000 years ago to today

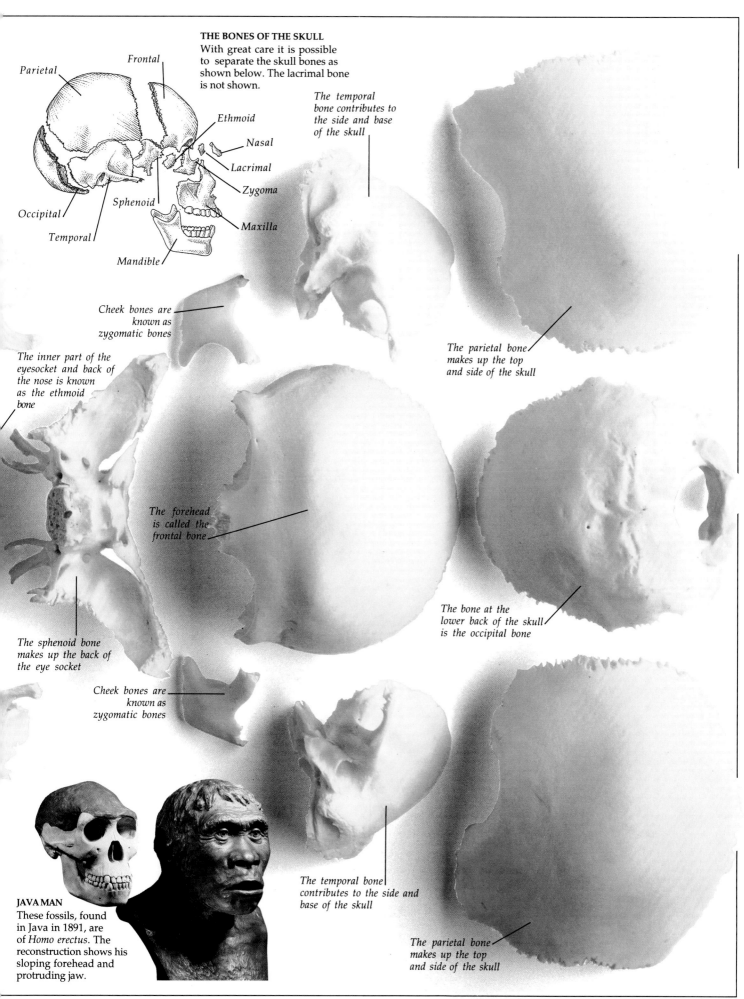

THE BONES OF THE SKULL
With great care it is possible
to separate the skull bones as
shown below. The lacrimal bone
is not shown.

Parietal

Frontal

Ethmoid

Nasal

Lacrimal

Zygoma

Maxilla

Occipital

Sphenoid

Temporal

Mandible

*The temporal
bone contributes to
the side and base
of the skull*

*Cheek bones are
known as
zygomatic bones*

*The parietal bone
makes up the top
and side of the skull*

*The inner part of the
eyesocket and back of
the nose is known
as the ethmoid
bone*

*The forehead
is called the
frontal bone*

*The sphenoid bone
makes up the back of
the eye socket*

*The bone at the
lower back of the skull
is the occipital bone*

*Cheek bones are
known as
zygomatic bones*

JAVA MAN
These fossils, found
in Java in 1891, are
of *Homo erectus*. The
reconstruction shows his
sloping forehead and
protruding jaw.

*The temporal bone
contributes to the side and
base of the skull*

*The parietal bone
makes up the top
and side of the skull*

Animal skulls

EACH SPECIES OF ANIMAL has a characteristic skull shape, moulded by evolution to suit its particular way of life. Some skulls are light, with weight-saving gaps, whereas others are thick and strong. Some are long and pointed, for probing and poking into holes, while others are short and broad. All the skulls shown here have jaws: this may not seem very remarkable, but, in fact, jaws were a great step forward when they first evolved, in fish about 450 million years ago. They enabled their owners to catch large chunks of food and break them into pieces small enough to swallow. Before this, fish were jawless and restricted to sucking or sieving food from the mud.

BIRDS AND BILLS
The typical bird skull is very light, with large eye sockets and a small, rounded case to the rear for the brain.

GANNET
A powerful bird with a long, streamlined bill, it dives from on high for fish.

AVOCET
Upturned bill for sieving seawater.

TAWNY OWL
Wide skull to house enormous eyes.

AMAZON PARROT
A massive hooked bill shows its seed-cracking power.

MERGANSER
This duck's serrated bill grasps fish to eat.

BLACKBIRD
All-purpose bill for eating insects, worms, berries and seeds.

CURLEW
Long bill probes for small creatures.

RABBIT
Its eyes are on the sides of its head, keeping an all-round watch for predators.

MALLARD
Wide, flattened bill "dabbles" in water for tiny bits of food.

HAMSTER
Gnaws at seeds and nuts with its large front teeth.

HEDGEHOG
Many, but similar, teeth indicate a diet of insects and other small animals.

THE LONG AND THE SHORT
In most kinds, or species, of animals, all individuals have a skull of much the same shape. All domestic dogs are one species, *Canis familiaris*. But over the centuries, people have selectively bred them for different features (below). Some have large, long skulls (usually working dogs) while smaller breeds tend to be more "decorative".

FROG
Forward-facing eyes judge distance of prey for accurate hunting.

ARMADILLO
The long nose sniffs out ants and other small creatures.

BADGER
Squat, heavy skull with long canine teeth point to a hunting way of life.

BOXER
Selective breeding has given the boxer a squashed-up snout, bringing the lower jaw to the front.

Protruding lower jaw

COLLIE
This breed has the more "natural" long muzzle of the dog's ancestor, the wolf.

Long muzzle

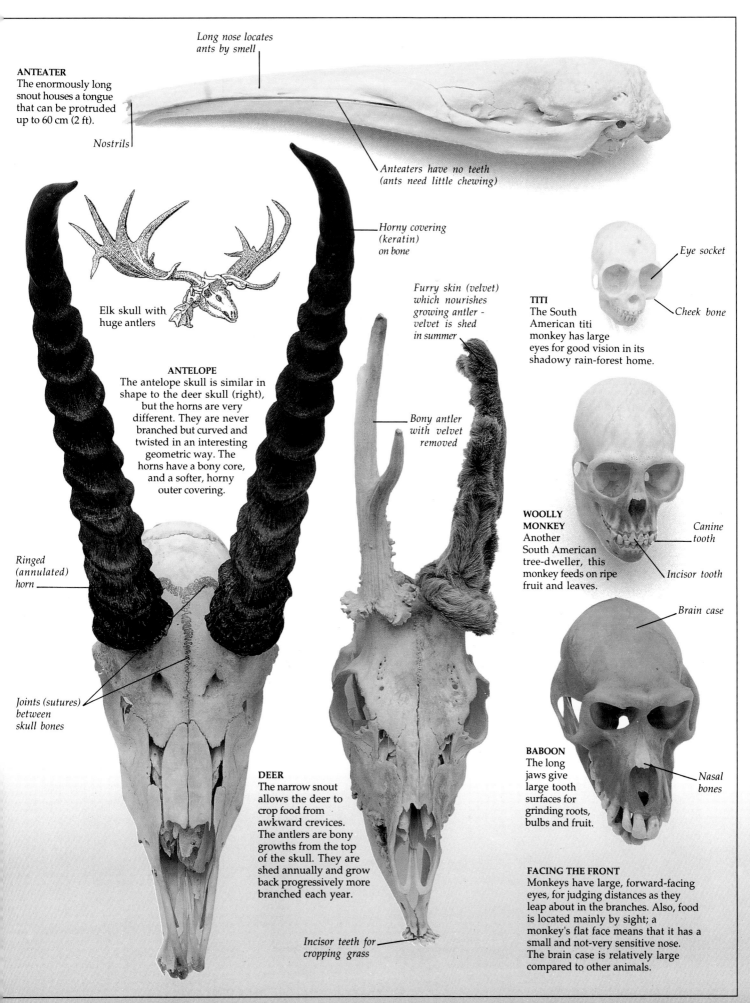

ANTEATER
The enormously long snout houses a tongue that can be protruded up to 60 cm (2 ft).

Long nose locates ants by smell

Nostrils

Anteaters have no teeth (ants need little chewing)

Horny covering (keratin) on bone

Elk skull with huge antlers

ANTELOPE
The antelope skull is similar in shape to the deer skull (right), but the horns are very different. They are never branched but curved and twisted in an interesting geometric way. The horns have a bony core, and a softer, horny outer covering.

Ringed (annulated) horn

Joints (sutures) between skull bones

Furry skin (velvet) which nourishes growing antler - velvet is shed in summer

Bony antler with velvet removed

TITI
The South American titi monkey has large eyes for good vision in its shadowy rain-forest home.

Eye socket

Cheek bone

WOOLLY MONKEY
Another South American tree-dweller, this monkey feeds on ripe fruit and leaves.

Canine tooth

Incisor tooth

Brain case

DEER
The narrow snout allows the deer to crop food from awkward crevices. The antlers are bony growths from the top of the skull. They are shed annually and grow back progressively more branched each year.

Incisor teeth for cropping grass

BABOON
The long jaws give large tooth surfaces for grinding roots, bulbs and fruit.

Nasal bones

FACING THE FRONT
Monkeys have large, forward-facing eyes, for judging distances as they leap about in the branches. Also, food is located mainly by sight; a monkey's flat face means that it has a small and not-very sensitive nose. The brain case is relatively large compared to other animals.

Animal senses

AN ANIMAL SKULL, like the other parts of the skeleton, is moulded by evolution. It is a concentrated collection of clues about how a creature lives and feeds. The skull's shape and size, particularly the parts dealing with the special senses - sight, hearing, smell and taste - are a result of adaptations to a particular lifestyle. A meat-eater that hunts mainly by sight tends to have large eyes, and therefore large eye sockets in its skull. An animal that hunts by scent develops a long snout, to house the enlarged organs of smell. Jaws and teeth are also very revealing, as described on pages 34-5.

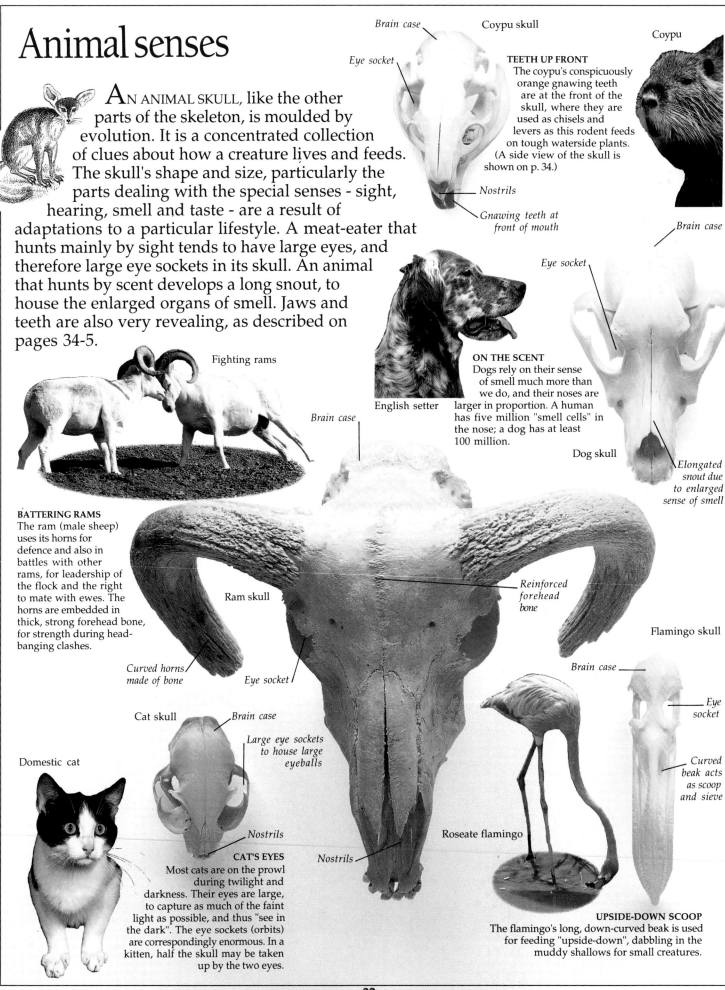

Brain case

Coypu skull

Eye socket

Coypu

TEETH UP FRONT
The coypu's conspicuously orange gnawing teeth are at the front of the skull, where they are used as chisels and levers as this rodent feeds on tough waterside plants. (A side view of the skull is shown on p. 34.)

Nostrils

Gnawing teeth at front of mouth

Brain case

Eye socket

English setter

ON THE SCENT
Dogs rely on their sense of smell much more than we do, and their noses are larger in proportion. A human has five million "smell cells" in the nose; a dog has at least 100 million.

Dog skull

Elongated snout due to enlarged sense of smell

Fighting rams

Brain case

BATTERING RAMS
The ram (male sheep) uses its horns for defence and also in battles with other rams, for leadership of the flock and the right to mate with ewes. The horns are embedded in thick, strong forehead bone, for strength during head-banging clashes.

Ram skull

Reinforced forehead bone

Flamingo skull

Brain case

Curved horns made of bone

Eye socket

Cat skull

Brain case

Large eye sockets to house large eyeballs

Eye socket

Curved beak acts as scoop and sieve

Domestic cat

Nostrils

CAT'S EYES
Most cats are on the prowl during twilight and darkness. Their eyes are large, to capture as much of the faint light as possible, and thus "see in the dark". The eye sockets (orbits) are correspondingly enormous. In a kitten, half the skull may be taken up by the two eyes.

Nostrils

Roseate flamingo

UPSIDE-DOWN SCOOP
The flamingo's long, down-curved beak is used for feeding "upside-down", dabbling in the muddy shallows for small creatures.

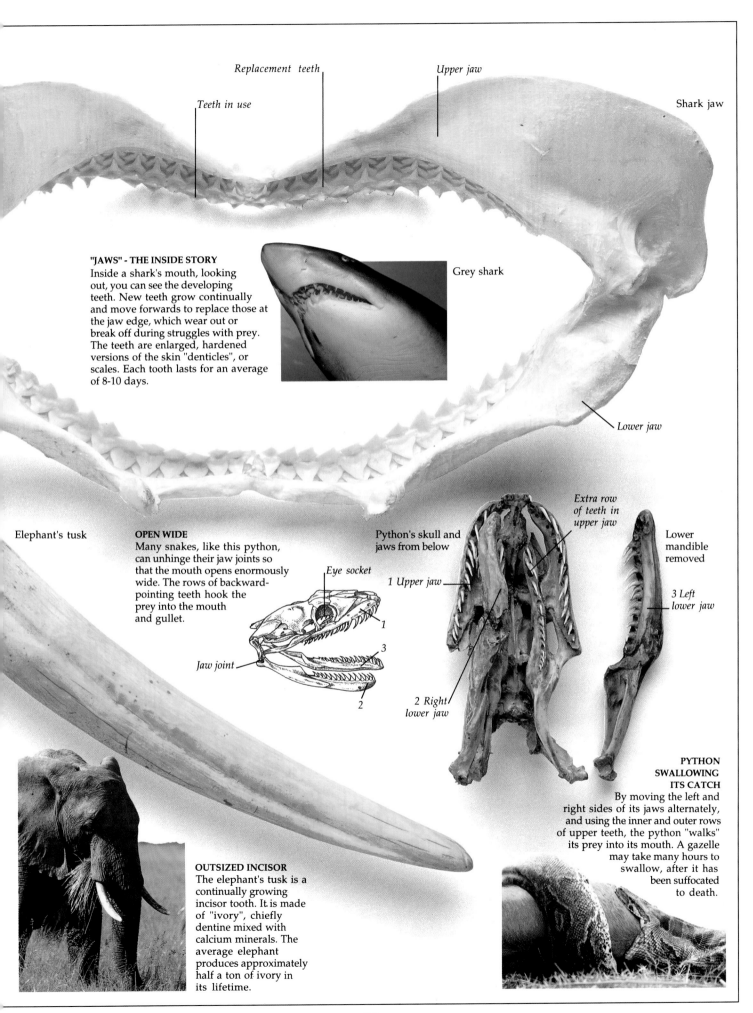

Replacement teeth

Upper jaw

Teeth in use

Shark jaw

"JAWS" - THE INSIDE STORY
Inside a shark's mouth, looking out, you can see the developing teeth. New teeth grow continually and move forwards to replace those at the jaw edge, which wear out or break off during struggles with prey. The teeth are enlarged, hardened versions of the skin "denticles", or scales. Each tooth lasts for an average of 8-10 days.

Grey shark

Lower jaw

Elephant's tusk

OPEN WIDE
Many snakes, like this python, can unhinge their jaw joints so that the mouth opens enormously wide. The rows of backward-pointing teeth hook the prey into the mouth and gullet.

Python's skull and jaws from below

Extra row of teeth in upper jaw

Lower mandible removed

Eye socket

1 Upper jaw

3 Left lower jaw

1

3

Jaw joint

2

2 Right lower jaw

PYTHON SWALLOWING ITS CATCH
By moving the left and right sides of its jaws alternately, and using the inner and outer rows of upper teeth, the python "walks" its prey into its mouth. A gazelle may take many hours to swallow, after it has been suffocated to death.

OUTSIZED INCISOR
The elephant's tusk is a continually growing incisor tooth. It is made of "ivory", chiefly dentine mixed with calcium minerals. The average elephant produces approximately half a ton of ivory in its lifetime.

The human spine

THE SPINE is literally the "back bone" of the human body. It forms a vertical supporting rod for the head, arms and legs. It allows us to stoop and squat, to turn and nod the head, and to twist the shoulders and hips. Yet it was originally designed as a horizontal girder, to take the weight of the chest and abdomen: the original prehistoric mammals almost certainly moved on all fours (p. 46). In the upright human, the spine has an S-shaped curve when seen from the side, to balance the various parts of the body over the legs and feet, so minimizing muscle strain when standing. The human spine works on the chain-link principle: many small movements add up. Each vertebra can only move a little in relation to its neighbours. But over the whole row this means the back can bend double. The spine shown below is "lying on its side", with the head end to the left and the "tail" on the right.

This engraving, from an anatomy book of 1685, features a back view of the human skeleton

THE CURVED SPINE *above*
From the side, the spine has a slight S-shape. This helps to bring the centres of gravity of the head, arms, chest and abdomen above the legs, so that the body as a whole is well balanced.

BELOW THE SKULL
The first two vertebrae are called the atlas and axis. All of the upper spine contributes to head movements, but these top two vertebrae are specialized to allow the head to nod and twist.

Atlas allows nodding movements

Axis allows side-to-side movements

IN THE NECK
There are seven vertebrae in the neck, called the cervical vertebrae. They allow us to turn our head in roughly three-quarters of a circle without moving the shoulders. (By moving our eyes as well, we can see in a complete circle.) Muscles run from the "wings" (transverse processes and neural spine) on the sides and rear of each vertebra to the skull, shoulder blades and lower vertebrae, to steady the head on the neck.

Cervical vertebra from behind

IN THE CHEST
The vertebrae become larger the lower they are in the spine, since they have to carry increasing weight. There are 12 chest (or thoracic) vertebrae, one for each pair of ribs. The ribs join to shallow cups on the body of the vertebra. The upper ten pairs of ribs also join to hollows on the transverse processes for extra stability. These two sets of joints move slightly every time you breathe.

Thoracic vertebra from behind

Shallow socket for end of rib

Body (centrum) of vertebra

Transverse process

Vertebral canal – hole for spinal cord

Transverse process

Cervical vertebra from top

Spine

Neural arch

Thoracic vertebra from top

Neural spine

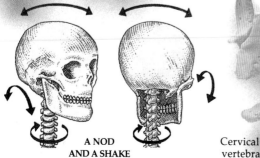

A NOD AND A SHAKE
The topmost vertebra, the atlas, allows nodding movements of the head. Side-to-side movements are a result of the atlas swivelling on the axis.

The protective role of the spine

The large holes in each vertebra line up to form a bony tunnel or canal. Inside this, well protected from knocks and twists, is the delicate spinal cord. Nerves enter and leave the cord through gaps between neighbouring vertebrae. Occasionally, a disc of cartilage between two vertebrae is squashed and presses on the nerve, causing the pain of a "slipped disc".

Spinal cord

Neural canal

Body of vertebra

Nerves to and from spinal cord

The delicate spinal cord runs through the neural canal of each vertebra

Brain

Nerves to upper body

Spinal cord

Nerves to lower body

Spine from front showing continuous column of vertebrae

A CONTINUOUS CANAL
The bones of the spine lie on top of each other to provide a continuous canal for the spinal cord. This cord emerges from the brain through a hole in the skull (p. 26), and the many nerves branch out from the canal through the gaps between neighbouring vertebrae.

SUPREME SUPPLENESS
The spine is most supple during our younger years, as this agile gymnast on the beam shows. As we grow older, extra knobs of bone grow on the vertebrae, and the cartilage discs between them become hardened. This reduces the spine's flexibility.

IN THE LOWER BACK
The five lumbar vertebrae carry the weight of the upper body. Their transverse processes and neural spines are correspondingly thicker, to anchor the large muscles that twist and bend the lower back. Between neighbouring vertebrae is a cushion-like disc of cartilage; the discs here are under greatest strain and may be ruptured or popped.

Lumbar vertebra from behind

Transverse process

Lumbar vertebra from top

IN THE HIPS
The rear part of the pelvis, the ring of bone in the hips, is formed by five vertebrae which have joined together during development. They form one solid bone called the sacrum. This sits, wedge-like, between the other parts of the pelvis (p. 44). The final part of the spine is the coccyx, or "tail bone", made from about four fused vertebrae.

Sacrum makes up part of the pelvis

Coccyx - the human "tail"

Body (centrum) of vertebra

Neural canal - hole for spinal cord

Neural spine

Neural arch

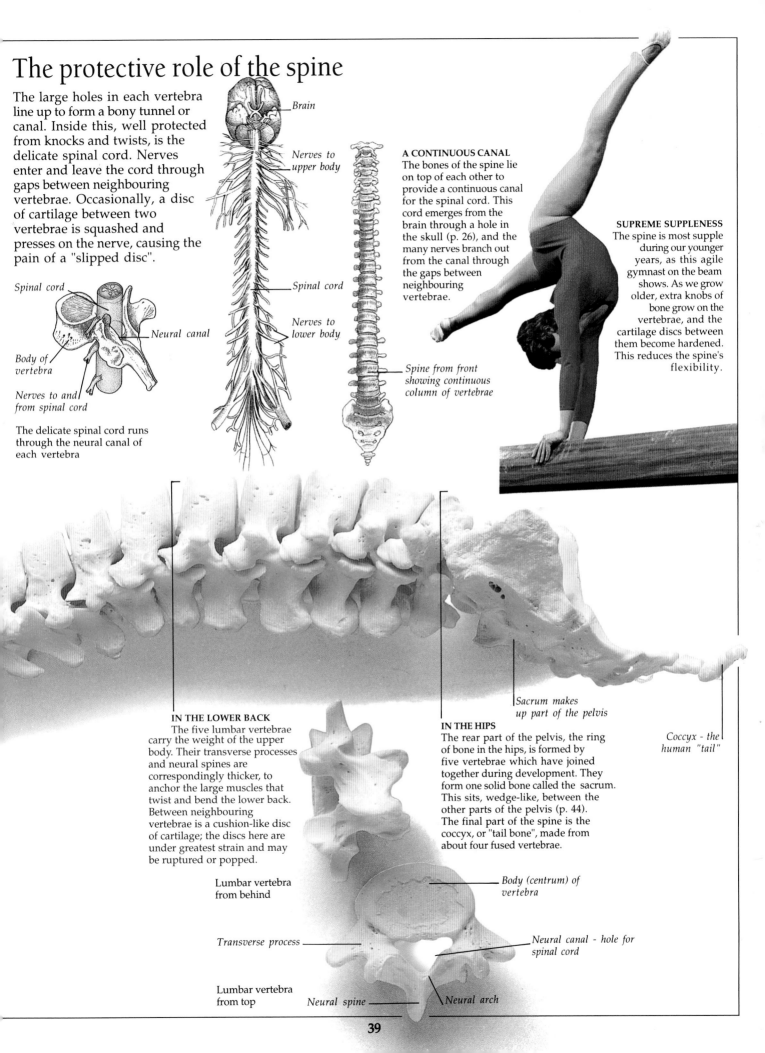

Animal backbones

EVERY FISH, REPTILE, amphibian, bird and mammal has a row of bones in its back, usually called the spine or spinal column. This is the feature that groups them together as vertebrates (animals with backbones or "vertebrae"), distinguishing them from invertebrates such as insects and worms (p. 22). The basic spine design is a row of small bones, linked together into a flexible column, with the skull at one end and a tail (usually) at the other. However, the number of individual vertebrae varies from as few as nine in a frog to more than 400 in some snakes!

A GRIPPING TAIL
The end of the lemur's spine - its tail - is prehensile and serves as a fifth limb, to grip branches while climbing. This also leaves both hands free when feeding.

Ring-tailed lemurs

Nose to tail length - 87 cm (35 in)

First two vertebrae allow head to twist and nod

HEAD TO TAIL
A fox has about 50 vertebrae, although around half of these are in its "brush" or tail. Those in the hip region have large flanges for the muscles and ligaments that secure the pelvis.

Region of stomach

Red fox

SLITHERING ALONG
In a snake each vertebra, with its pair of ribs, is virtually identical to all the others. A snake's skeleton is all backbone as it has no arms, legs, shoulder blades or pelvis. Large snakes, such as this python, use their belly scales to move. The scales, attached to the ribs, are pushed backwards in groups, their rear edges tilted down to grip the ground.

Shoulder blades linked here

Python skeleton

Reticulated python

Skull

Region of heart

Lower jaw

AGILE REPTILES
Lack of limbs does not seem to restrict snakes, such as this reticulated python. They can move very fast, climb, swim and burrow.

Rib

Region of intestine

Shark spinal column

Round discs
of cartilage

Grey shark

Neural spine anchors
muscles that force tail
upwards, moving
whale forwards

Forward-pointing
transverse processes
fit into grooves of
vertebra in front

SHARK SPINE
A shark's "backbones" are not bone at all
(and neither is the rest of the
skeleton). They are made mainly
of cartilage (gristle). The
central part of each one,
the centrum, as shown
here, is hardened
with minerals such
as calcium.

Strengthening "spokes"
of hard minerals

Individual vertebrae
Take a spine apart, and the
general shape of each vertebra
becomes clear. The rounded lump
of bone, the centrum, butts up against
its neighbours fore and aft. Above
this is a hole, the neural canal,
through which runs the well-
protected spinal nerve cord. The
"wings" of bone (transverse processes)
anchor muscles that move the back
and, in a four-legged creature,
support the underslung
weight of the body.

Hole for
spinal cord
is called
the neural canal

Hips attach to sacrum
(fused vertebrae)

Neural
spine

Fox spinal
column

Neural
spine

Centrum

Ferret vertebra

Neural arch

Neural canal

RUNNER AND SWIMMER
The dolphin's vertebra has
relatively large bony wings for
anchoring the back-bending muscles,
compared with the ferret's tiny
equivalents. This is because a dolphin
swims entirely by undulations of its
spine, while the ferret, although a
sinuous mover, relies more on
its leg muscles.

Transverse
process

Centrum

Dolphin vertebra

Baleen whale
vertebra

Transverse process

THE LARGEST MAMMAL
This rear view of a whale vertebra
shows the system of pegs and grooves
that stop the spine twisting too much.
The forward-pointing transverse
processes fit into grooves in the vertebra
in front; similar transverse processes from
the vertebra behind fit into the grooves
on this vertebra.

The rib cage

PROBLEM: the lungs need to inflate and deflate, becoming larger and smaller as they breathe; yet they also need protection against being knocked or crushed. A solid case of protective bone, like the skull around the brain, would be too rigid. Answer: a flexible cage with moveable bars - the ribs. Closely spaced, with tough ligaments and muscles between them, the ribs give good protection to the delicate lungs. In addition, each rib is thin and flexible, so that it can absorb knocks without cracking and puncturing the vital airtight seal around the lungs. The ribs move at the points where they join the spine and breastbone. When breathing in, muscles lift the ribs upwards and swing them outwards, increasing the volume of the chest and sucking air into the lungs.

Breastbone

Inside the chest

The ribs protect the lungs and also the other organs in the chest, such as the heart and main blood vessels. And they guard the stomach, liver and other parts of the upper abdomen. These organs nestle under the diaphragm, a dome-shaped muscle that forms the base of the chest, so they are above the level of the bottom ribs.

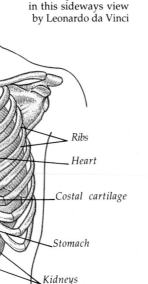

The depth of the rib cage and its relation to the spine is shown in this sideways view by Leonardo da Vinci

Collar bone

Lungs

Breastbone

Liver

Ribs

Heart

Costal cartilage

Stomach

Kidneys

A CAGE OF BONY BARS
The chest cage is made up of the spine at the back, 12 pairs of ribs arched around the sides, and the breastbone in front.

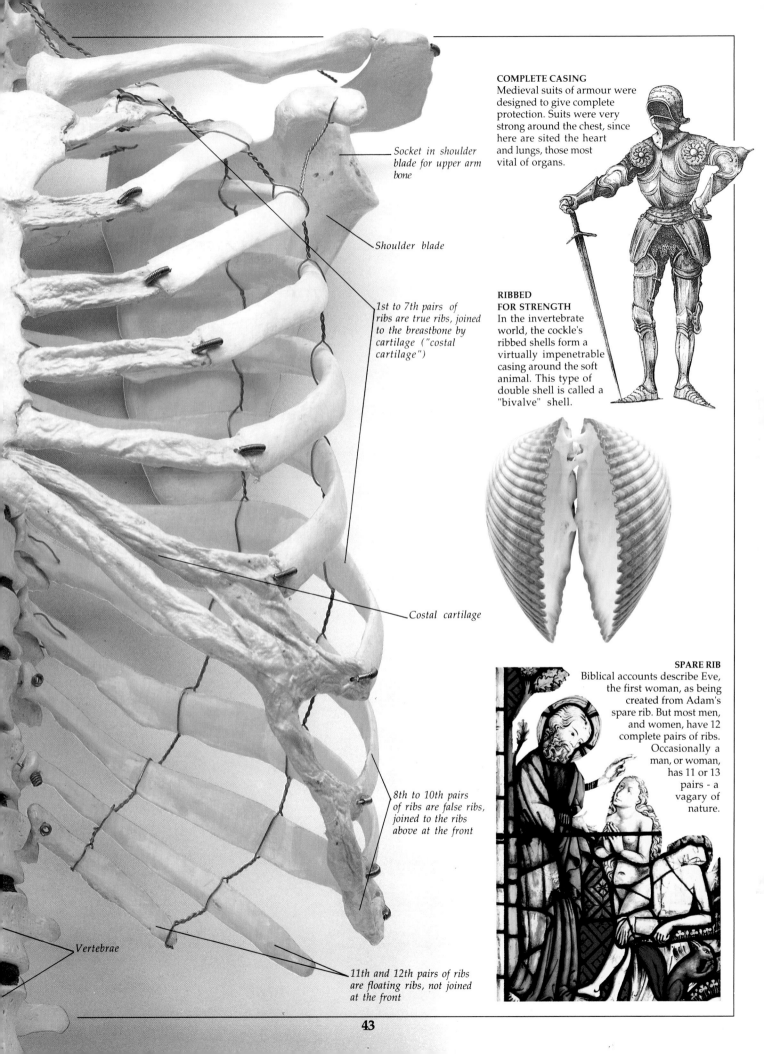

Socket in shoulder blade for upper arm bone

Shoulder blade

1st to 7th pairs of ribs are true ribs, joined to the breastbone by cartilage ("costal cartilage")

Costal cartilage

8th to 10th pairs of ribs are false ribs, joined to the ribs above at the front

Vertebrae

11th and 12th pairs of ribs are floating ribs, not joined at the front

COMPLETE CASING
Medieval suits of armour were designed to give complete protection. Suits were very strong around the chest, since here are sited the heart and lungs, those most vital of organs.

RIBBED FOR STRENGTH
In the invertebrate world, the cockle's ribbed shells form a virtually impenetrable casing around the soft animal. This type of double shell is called a "bivalve" shell.

SPARE RIB
Biblical accounts describe Eve, the first woman, as being created from Adam's spare rib. But most men, and women, have 12 complete pairs of ribs. Occasionally a man, or woman, has 11 or 13 pairs - a vagary of nature.

Human hip bones

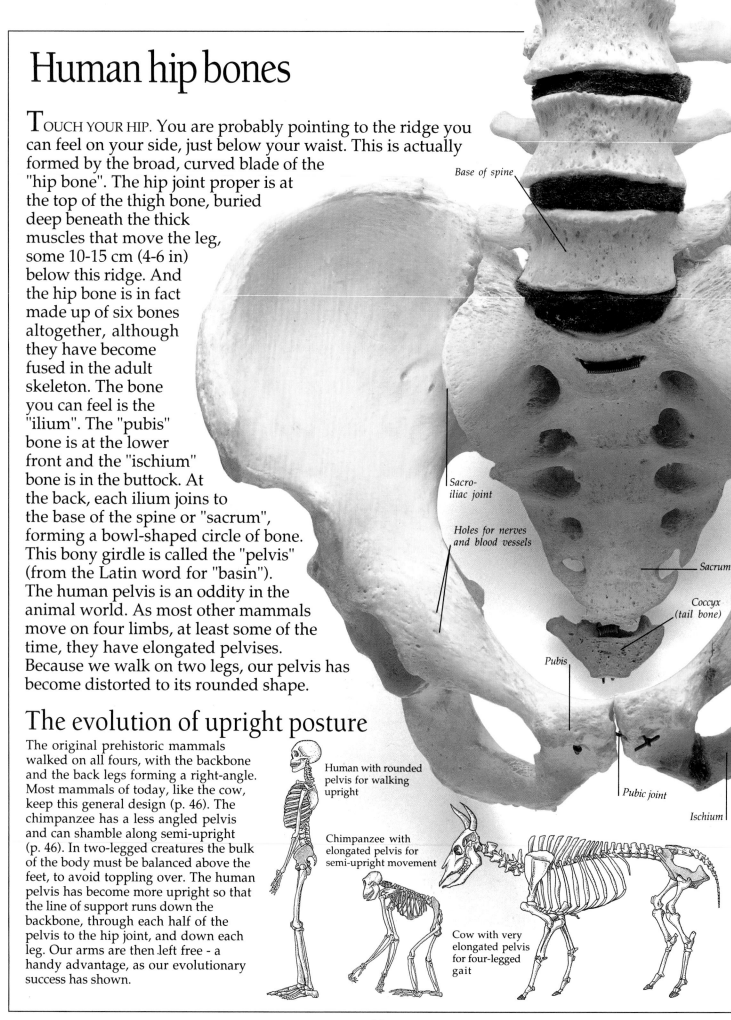

TOUCH YOUR HIP. You are probably pointing to the ridge you can feel on your side, just below your waist. This is actually formed by the broad, curved blade of the "hip bone". The hip joint proper is at the top of the thigh bone, buried deep beneath the thick muscles that move the leg, some 10-15 cm (4-6 in) below this ridge. And the hip bone is in fact made up of six bones altogether, although they have become fused in the adult skeleton. The bone you can feel is the "ilium". The "pubis" bone is at the lower front and the "ischium" bone is in the buttock. At the back, each ilium joins to the base of the spine or "sacrum", forming a bowl-shaped circle of bone. This bony girdle is called the "pelvis" (from the Latin word for "basin"). The human pelvis is an oddity in the animal world. As most other mammals move on four limbs, at least some of the time, they have elongated pelvises. Because we walk on two legs, our pelvis has become distorted to its rounded shape.

Base of spine

Sacro-iliac joint

Holes for nerves and blood vessels

Sacrum

Coccyx (tail bone)

Pubis

Pubic joint

Ischium

The evolution of upright posture

The original prehistoric mammals walked on all fours, with the backbone and the back legs forming a right-angle. Most mammals of today, like the cow, keep this general design (p. 46). The chimpanzee has a less angled pelvis and can shamble along semi-upright (p. 46). In two-legged creatures the bulk of the body must be balanced above the feet, to avoid toppling over. The human pelvis has become more upright so that the line of support runs down the backbone, through each half of the pelvis to the hip joint, and down each leg. Our arms are then left free - a handy advantage, as our evolutionary success has shown.

Human with rounded pelvis for walking upright

Chimpanzee with elongated pelvis for semi-upright movement

Cow with very elongated pelvis for four-legged gait

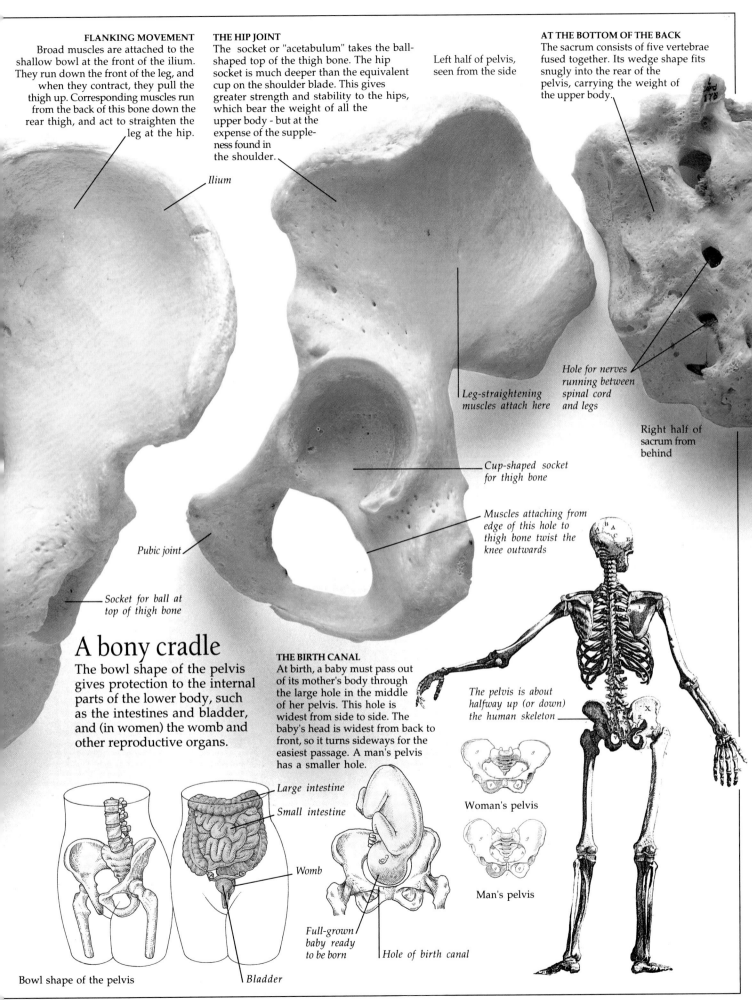

FLANKING MOVEMENT
Broad muscles are attached to the shallow bowl at the front of the ilium. They run down the front of the leg, and when they contract, they pull the thigh up. Corresponding muscles run from the back of this bone down the rear thigh, and act to straighten the leg at the hip.

Ilium

THE HIP JOINT
The socket or "acetabulum" takes the ball-shaped top of the thigh bone. The hip socket is much deeper than the equivalent cup on the shoulder blade. This gives greater strength and stability to the hips, which bear the weight of all the upper body - but at the expense of the suppleness found in the shoulder.

Left half of pelvis, seen from the side

AT THE BOTTOM OF THE BACK
The sacrum consists of five vertebrae fused together. Its wedge shape fits snugly into the rear of the pelvis, carrying the weight of the upper body.

Leg-straightening muscles attach here

Hole for nerves running between spinal cord and legs

Cup-shaped socket for thigh bone

Right half of sacrum from behind

Muscles attaching from edge of this hole to thigh bone twist the knee outwards

Pubic joint

Socket for ball at top of thigh bone

A bony cradle
The bowl shape of the pelvis gives protection to the internal parts of the lower body, such as the intestines and bladder, and (in women) the womb and other reproductive organs.

THE BIRTH CANAL
At birth, a baby must pass out of its mother's body through the large hole in the middle of her pelvis. This hole is widest from side to side. The baby's head is widest from back to front, so it turns sideways for the easiest passage. A man's pelvis has a smaller hole.

The pelvis is about halfway up (or down) the human skeleton

Large intestine

Small intestine

Womb

Bladder

Full-grown baby ready to be born

Hole of birth canal

Bowl shape of the pelvis

Woman's pelvis

Man's pelvis

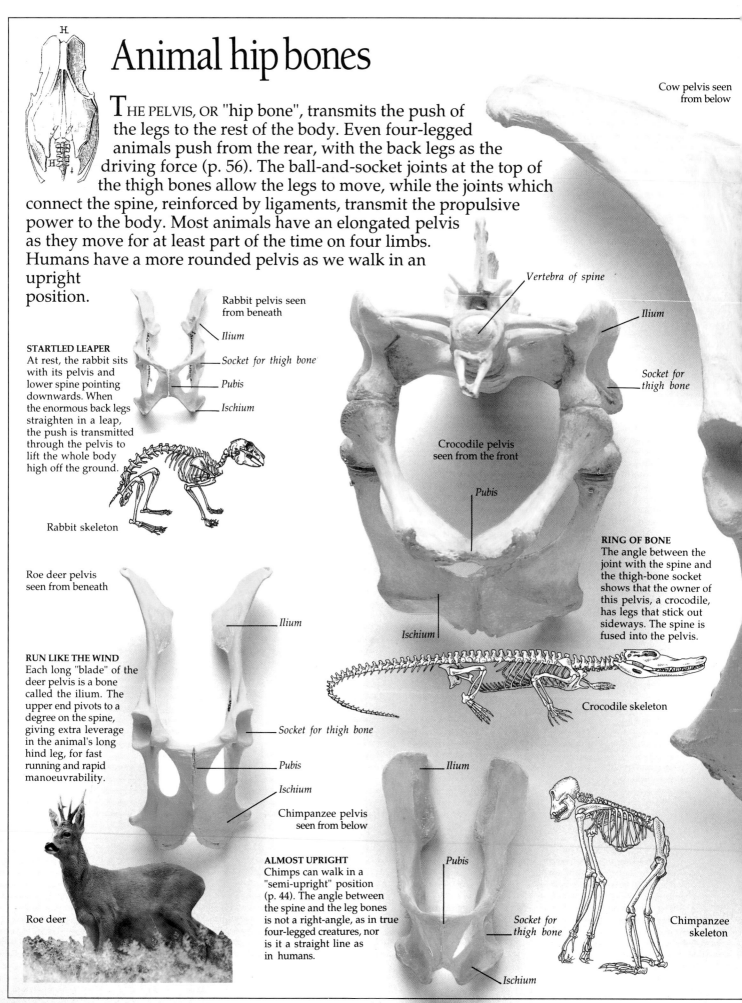

Animal hip bones

Cow pelvis seen from below

THE PELVIS, OR "hip bone", transmits the push of the legs to the rest of the body. Even four-legged animals push from the rear, with the back legs as the driving force (p. 56). The ball-and-socket joints at the top of the thigh bones allow the legs to move, while the joints which connect the spine, reinforced by ligaments, transmit the propulsive power to the body. Most animals have an elongated pelvis as they move for at least part of the time on four limbs. Humans have a more rounded pelvis as we walk in an upright position.

Rabbit pelvis seen from beneath

Ilium

Socket for thigh bone

Pubis

Ischium

STARTLED LEAPER
At rest, the rabbit sits with its pelvis and lower spine pointing downwards. When the enormous back legs straighten in a leap, the push is transmitted through the pelvis to lift the whole body high off the ground.

Rabbit skeleton

Vertebra of spine

Ilium

Socket for thigh bone

Crocodile pelvis seen from the front

Pubis

Roe deer pelvis seen from beneath

Ilium

RUN LIKE THE WIND
Each long "blade" of the deer pelvis is a bone called the ilium. The upper end pivots to a degree on the spine, giving extra leverage in the animal's long hind leg, for fast running and rapid manoeuvrability.

Socket for thigh bone

Pubis

Ischium

Ischium

RING OF BONE
The angle between the joint with the spine and the thigh-bone socket shows that the owner of this pelvis, a crocodile, has legs that stick out sideways. The spine is fused into the pelvis.

Crocodile skeleton

Chimpanzee pelvis seen from below

Ilium

Pubis

ALMOST UPRIGHT
Chimps can walk in a "semi-upright" position (p. 44). The angle between the spine and the leg bones is not a right-angle, as in true four-legged creatures, nor is it a straight line as in humans.

Roe deer

Socket for thigh bone

Ischium

Chimpanzee skeleton

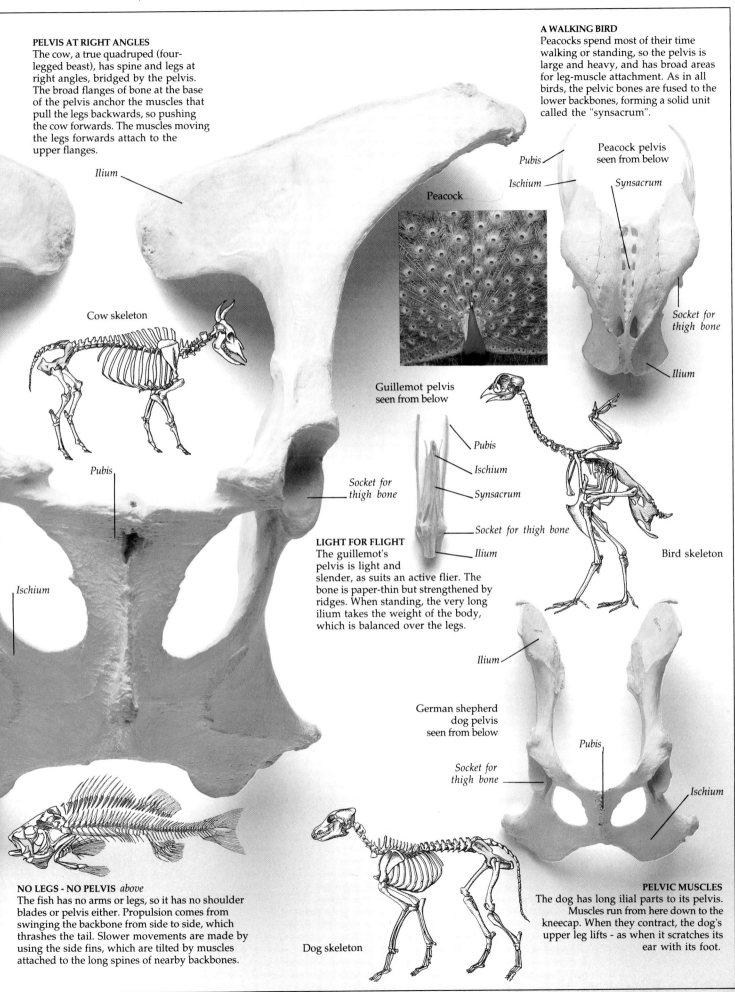

PELVIS AT RIGHT ANGLES
The cow, a true quadruped (four-legged beast), has spine and legs at right angles, bridged by the pelvis. The broad flanges of bone at the base of the pelvis anchor the muscles that pull the legs backwards, so pushing the cow forwards. The muscles moving the legs forwards attach to the upper flanges.

Ilium

Cow skeleton

Pubis

Ischium

A WALKING BIRD
Peacocks spend most of their time walking or standing, so the pelvis is large and heavy, and has broad areas for leg-muscle attachment. As in all birds, the pelvic bones are fused to the lower backbones, forming a solid unit called the "synsacrum".

Peacock

Pubis

Peacock pelvis
seen from below

Ischium

Synsacrum

*Socket for
thigh bone*

Ilium

Guillemot pelvis
seen from below

*Socket for
thigh bone*

Pubis

Ischium

Synsacrum

Socket for thigh bone

Ilium

LIGHT FOR FLIGHT
The guillemot's pelvis is light and slender, as suits an active flier. The bone is paper-thin but strengthened by ridges. When standing, the very long ilium takes the weight of the body, which is balanced over the legs.

Bird skeleton

Ilium

German shepherd
dog pelvis
seen from below

*Socket for
thigh bone*

Pubis

Ischium

NO LEGS - NO PELVIS *above*
The fish has no arms or legs, so it has no shoulder blades or pelvis either. Propulsion comes from swinging the backbone from side to side, which thrashes the tail. Slower movements are made by using the side fins, which are tilted by muscles attached to the long spines of nearby backbones.

Dog skeleton

PELVIC MUSCLES
The dog has long ilial parts to its pelvis. Muscles run from here down to the kneecap. When they contract, the dog's upper leg lifts - as when it scratches its ear with its foot.

The human arm and hand

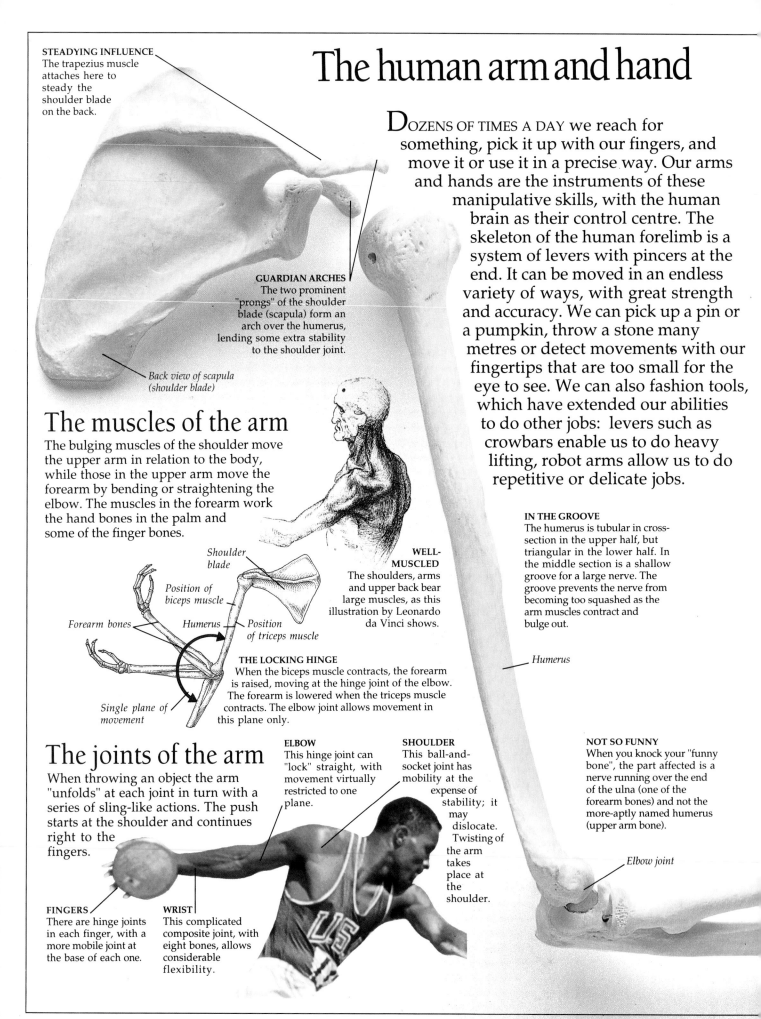

STEADYING INFLUENCE
The trapezius muscle attaches here to steady the shoulder blade on the back.

GUARDIAN ARCHES
The two prominent "prongs" of the shoulder blade (scapula) form an arch over the humerus, lending some extra stability to the shoulder joint.

Back view of scapula (shoulder blade)

DOZENS OF TIMES A DAY we reach for something, pick it up with our fingers, and move it or use it in a precise way. Our arms and hands are the instruments of these manipulative skills, with the human brain as their control centre. The skeleton of the human forelimb is a system of levers with pincers at the end. It can be moved in an endless variety of ways, with great strength and accuracy. We can pick up a pin or a pumpkin, throw a stone many metres or detect movements with our fingertips that are too small for the eye to see. We can also fashion tools, which have extended our abilities to do other jobs: levers such as crowbars enable us to do heavy lifting, robot arms allow us to do repetitive or delicate jobs.

The muscles of the arm

The bulging muscles of the shoulder move the upper arm in relation to the body, while those in the upper arm move the forearm by bending or straightening the elbow. The muscles in the forearm work the hand bones in the palm and some of the finger bones.

Shoulder blade

Position of biceps muscle

Forearm bones

Humerus

Position of triceps muscle

Single plane of movement

WELL-MUSCLED
The shoulders, arms and upper back bear large muscles, as this illustration by Leonardo da Vinci shows.

THE LOCKING HINGE
When the biceps muscle contracts, the forearm is raised, moving at the hinge joint of the elbow. The forearm is lowered when the triceps muscle contracts. The elbow joint allows movement in this plane only.

IN THE GROOVE
The humerus is tubular in cross-section in the upper half, but triangular in the lower half. In the middle section is a shallow groove for a large nerve. The groove prevents the nerve from becoming too squashed as the arm muscles contract and bulge out.

Humerus

The joints of the arm

When throwing an object the arm "unfolds" at each joint in turn with a series of sling-like actions. The push starts at the shoulder and continues right to the fingers.

ELBOW
This hinge joint can "lock" straight, with movement virtually restricted to one plane.

SHOULDER
This ball-and-socket joint has mobility at the expense of stability; it may dislocate. Twisting of the arm takes place at the shoulder.

NOT SO FUNNY
When you knock your "funny bone", the part affected is a nerve running over the end of the ulna (one of the forearm bones) and not the more-aptly named humerus (upper arm bone).

Elbow joint

FINGERS
There are hinge joints in each finger, with a more mobile joint at the base of each one.

WRIST
This complicated composite joint, with eight bones, allows considerable flexibility.

The bones of the hand

Our hands are built on the standard mammal five-digit plan. Why the "magic number" should be five is not really known. The wrist bones provide anchorage for the small muscles that help to move the thumb and fingers. Other finger-moving muscles are in the forearm, connected to the fingers by long tendons that run through a "collar" of ligaments in the wrist.

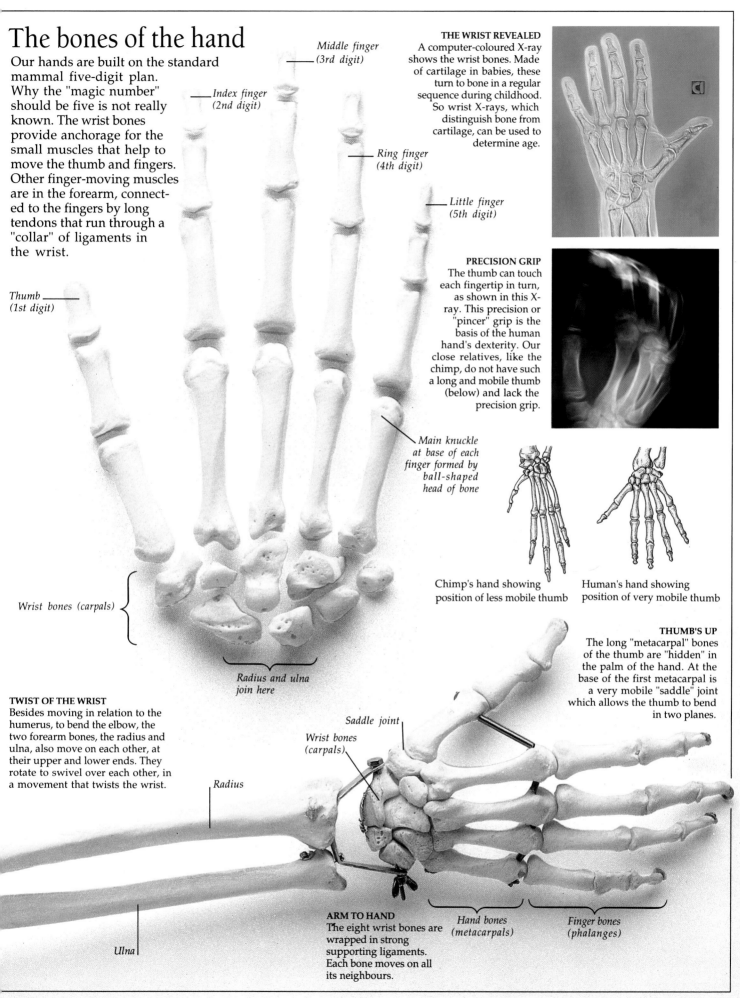

Middle finger
(3rd digit)

Index finger
(2nd digit)

Ring finger
(4th digit)

Little finger
(5th digit)

Thumb
(1st digit)

Main knuckle
at base of each
finger formed by
ball-shaped
head of bone

Wrist bones (carpals)

Radius and ulna
join here

THE WRIST REVEALED
A computer-coloured X-ray shows the wrist bones. Made of cartilage in babies, these turn to bone in a regular sequence during childhood. So wrist X-rays, which distinguish bone from cartilage, can be used to determine age.

PRECISION GRIP
The thumb can touch each fingertip in turn, as shown in this X-ray. This precision or "pincer" grip is the basis of the human hand's dexterity. Our close relatives, like the chimp, do not have such a long and mobile thumb (below) and lack the precision grip.

Chimp's hand showing
position of less mobile thumb

Human's hand showing
position of very mobile thumb

THUMB'S UP
The long "metacarpal" bones of the thumb are "hidden" in the palm of the hand. At the base of the first metacarpal is a very mobile "saddle" joint which allows the thumb to bend in two planes.

TWIST OF THE WRIST
Besides moving in relation to the humerus, to bend the elbow, the two forearm bones, the radius and ulna, also move on each other, at their upper and lower ends. They rotate to swivel over each other, in a movement that twists the wrist.

Saddle joint

Wrist bones
(carpals)

Radius

Ulna

ARM TO HAND
The eight wrist bones are wrapped in strong supporting ligaments. Each bone moves on all its neighbours.

Hand bones
(metacarpals)

Finger bones
(phalanges)

Arms, wings and flippers

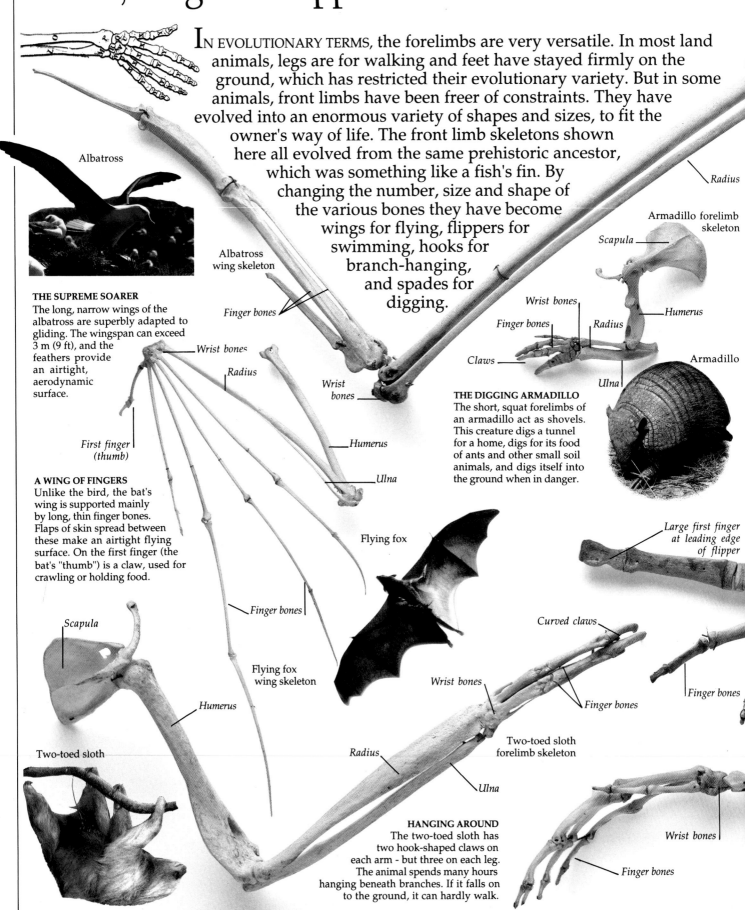

IN EVOLUTIONARY TERMS, the forelimbs are very versatile. In most land animals, legs are for walking and feet have stayed firmly on the ground, which has restricted their evolutionary variety. But in some animals, front limbs have been freer of constraints. They have evolved into an enormous variety of shapes and sizes, to fit the owner's way of life. The front limb skeletons shown here all evolved from the same prehistoric ancestor, which was something like a fish's fin. By changing the number, size and shape of the various bones they have become wings for flying, flippers for swimming, hooks for branch-hanging, and spades for digging.

Albatross

Albatross wing skeleton

Finger bones

THE SUPREME SOARER
The long, narrow wings of the albatross are superbly adapted to gliding. The wingspan can exceed 3 m (9 ft), and the feathers provide an airtight, aerodynamic surface.

Wrist bones

Radius

Wrist bones

First finger (thumb)

Humerus

Ulna

A WING OF FINGERS
Unlike the bird, the bat's wing is supported mainly by long, thin finger bones. Flaps of skin spread between these make an airtight flying surface. On the first finger (the bat's "thumb") is a claw, used for crawling or holding food.

Scapula

Humerus

Finger bones

Flying fox

Flying fox wing skeleton

Two-toed sloth

Radius

Ulna

Wrist bones

HANGING AROUND
The two-toed sloth has two hook-shaped claws on each arm - but three on each leg. The animal spends many hours hanging beneath branches. If it falls on to the ground, it can hardly walk.

Radius

Armadillo forelimb skeleton

Scapula

Wrist bones

Finger bones

Radius

Humerus

Claws

Armadillo

Ulna

THE DIGGING ARMADILLO
The short, squat forelimbs of an armadillo act as shovels. This creature digs a tunnel for a home, digs for its food of ants and other small soil animals, and digs itself into the ground when in danger.

Large first finger at leading edge of flipper

Curved claws

Finger bones

Finger bones

Two-toed sloth forelimb skeleton

Wrist bones

Finger bones

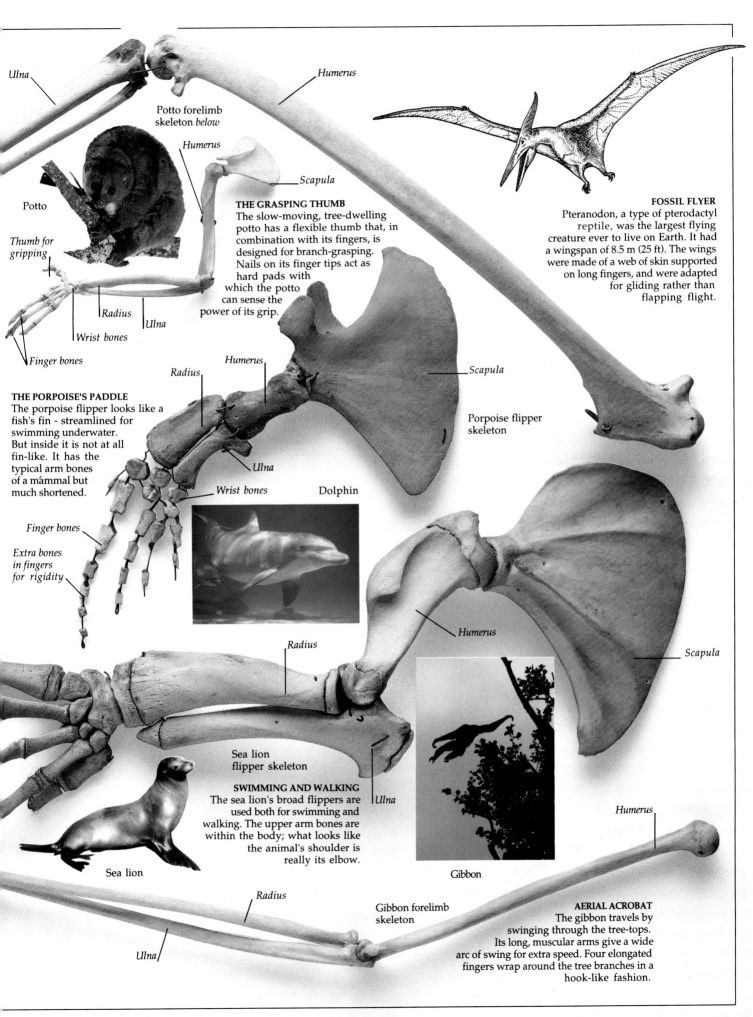

Ulna

Humerus

Potto forelimb
skeleton *below*

Humerus

Scapula

THE GRASPING THUMB
The slow-moving, tree-dwelling
potto has a flexible thumb that, in
combination with its fingers, is
designed for branch-grasping.
Nails on its finger tips act as
hard pads with
which the potto
can sense the
power of its grip.

Potto

*Thumb for
gripping*

Radius

Ulna

Wrist bones

Finger bones

THE PORPOISE'S PADDLE
The porpoise flipper looks like a
fish's fin - streamlined for
swimming underwater.
But inside it is not at all
fin-like. It has the
typical arm bones
of a mammal but
much shortened.

Radius

Humerus

Scapula

Ulna

Porpoise flipper
skeleton

Dolphin

Finger bones

*Extra bones
in fingers
for rigidity*

Radius

Humerus

Scapula

Sea lion
flipper skeleton

SWIMMING AND WALKING
The sea lion's broad flippers are
used both for swimming and
walking. The upper arm bones are
within the body; what looks like
the animal's shoulder is
really its elbow.

Ulna

Humerus

Sea lion

Gibbon

Radius

Gibbon forelimb
skeleton

AERIAL ACROBAT
The gibbon travels by
swinging through the tree-tops.
Its long, muscular arms give a wide
arc of swing for extra speed. Four elongated
fingers wrap around the tree branches in a
hook-like fashion.

Ulna

FOSSIL FLYER
Pteranodon, a type of pterodactyl
reptile, was the largest flying
creature ever to live on Earth. It had
a wingspan of 8.5 m (25 ft). The wings
were made of a web of skin supported
on long fingers, and were adapted
for gliding rather than
flapping flight.

Animal shoulder blades

FROM THE OUTSIDE, the four limbs of a four-legged animal look much the same. But inside, the skeleton reveals many differences. The back legs are designed mainly for propelling the whole body when walking, running or jumping (p. 56). The front legs, on the other hand, do various jobs. They cushion the body when landing after a leap; they may manipulate food or objects; and they can strike at prey or enemies. So they need to be more flexible. The key to their wider range of movement is the shoulder blade, or "scapula". This triangle of bone connects to the body chiefly by muscles that run to the backbone and ribs, and that can tilt it at many angles. And it links to the forelimb by a ball-and-socket joint, giving even greater suppleness.

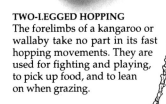
Red fox

Red fox shoulder blade

ON THE TROT
The fox's broad shoulder blade has a large surface area for muscle anchorage, indicating that it moves for much of the time on all fours. Foxes may also dig for food with their front legs.

Collared peccary shoulder blade

STIFF-LEGGED PIG
The long, narrow shoulder blade of the collared peccary, a type of pig, is swung forward and back by the muscles connecting it to the body. The legs are relatively short and thin, resulting in a rather stiff-legged walk.

Beaver holding twig it is gnawing

DAM-BUILDER
The beaver's smallish shoulder blade shows that its short front limbs are not weight-carriers. They are manipulators, for prodding twigs and mud into dams and holding food.

Pig skeleton

Wallaby shoulder blade

CROUCHING TO DRINK
A Siberian tiger lowers itself over a pool to drink. Its spine is lowered between its front legs, and the shoulder blades show clearly on each side of the body.

Beaver shoulder blade

TWO-LEGGED HOPPING
The forelimbs of a kangaroo or wallaby take no part in its fast hopping movements. They are used for fighting and playing, to pick up food, and to lean on when grazing.

Kangaroo skeleton

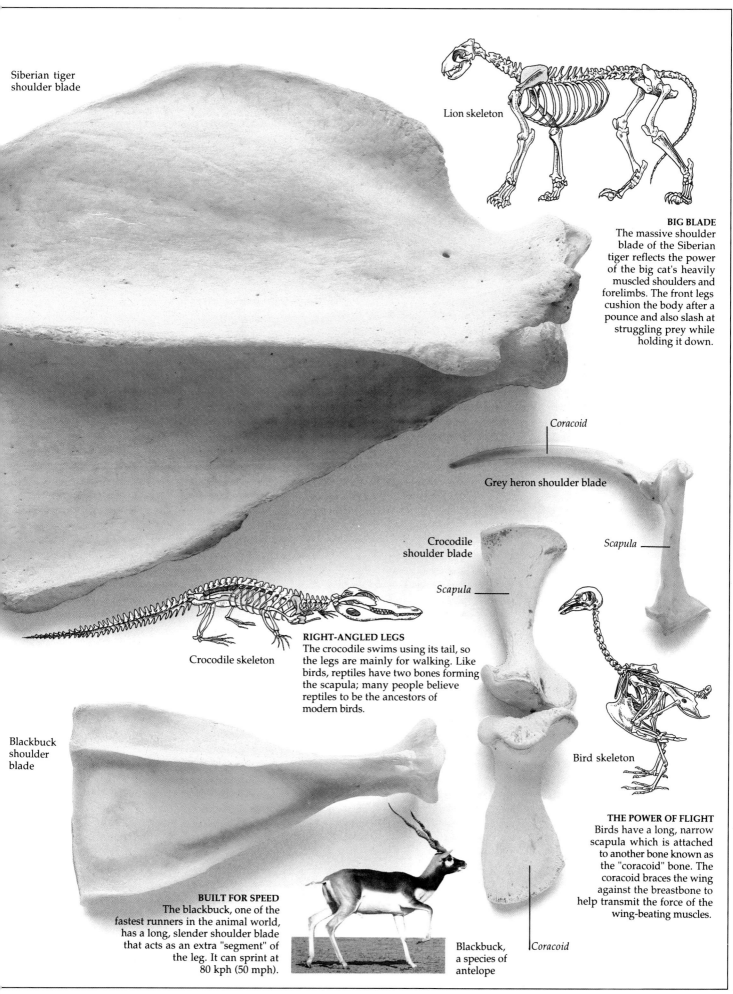

Siberian tiger
shoulder blade

Lion skeleton

BIG BLADE
The massive shoulder
blade of the Siberian
tiger reflects the power
of the big cat's heavily
muscled shoulders and
forelimbs. The front legs
cushion the body after a
pounce and also slash at
struggling prey while
holding it down.

Coracoid

Grey heron shoulder blade

Crocodile
shoulder blade

Scapula

Scapula

Crocodile skeleton

RIGHT-ANGLED LEGS
The crocodile swims using its tail, so
the legs are mainly for walking. Like
birds, reptiles have two bones forming
the scapula; many people believe
reptiles to be the ancestors of
modern birds.

Bird skeleton

Blackbuck
shoulder
blade

THE POWER OF FLIGHT
Birds have a long, narrow
scapula which is attached
to another bone known as
the "coracoid" bone. The
coracoid braces the wing
against the breastbone to
help transmit the force of the
wing-beating muscles.

BUILT FOR SPEED
The blackbuck, one of the
fastest runners in the animal world,
has a long, slender shoulder blade
that acts as an extra "segment" of
the leg. It can sprint at
80 kph (50 mph).

Blackbuck,
a species of
antelope

Coracoid

The human leg and foot

WE ARE SO used to standing and watching the world go by, that we are not usually aware of what an amazing balancing feat this is. Other animals may be able to stand on their back limbs temporarily, but they usually topple over after a few seconds. We can maintain a fully upright, two-legged posture for hours, leaving our arms and hands free for other tasks. Compared to the arm (p. 48), the bones of the human leg are thick and strong, to carry the body's weight. We do not walk on our toes, like many creatures (p. 56). Our feet are broad and also long, for good fore-aft stability, while our toes are much smaller than in most other animals. Small muscle adjustments take place continuously in the neck, arms, back and legs, keeping our weight over our feet. Walking requires the coordination and contraction of dozens of muscles. It has been called "controlled falling": the body tilts forwards, so that it begins to tip over, only to be saved from falling by moving a foot forwards.

Head of thigh bone

THE HEAD OF THE LEG
The thigh bone is the largest single bone in the body. At its top end, or "head", it is reinforced by ridges that anchor powerful leg-moving muscles.

LONG, YET STRONG
In accordance with good engineering design, the shaft of the thigh bone is long and tube-like. It is subjected to fewer stresses and strains along its length than at the ends.

SWINGING ARMS
As you walk, the arm on one side swings forwards as the leg on that side swings back. The two movements partly cancel each other out, keeping the weight of the body fairly central.

The muscles and joints of the leg

The muscles at the hip, thigh and calf move the limbs at the joints. Those at the hip swing the leg forwards and backwards at the hip joint, as when walking. The muscles at the back of the thigh bend the knee at its hinge joint. Those in the calf straighten the foot at the ankle joint.

MUSCLES FOR MOVING THE LEG
This rear view of the legs shows all the muscles important in movement.

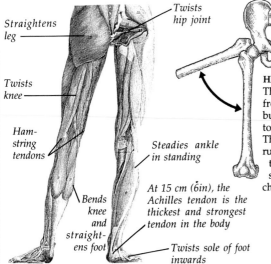

Straightens leg

Twists knee

Hamstring tendons

Bends knee and straightens foot

Twists hip joint

Steadies ankle in standing

At 15 cm (6in), the Achilles tendon is the thickest and strongest tendon in the body

Twists sole of foot inwards

HIP LIMITS
The hip has good front-to-back mobility but only limited side-to-side movement. The former is for running and walking; the latter for suddenly changing direction.

THE HIP
This ball-and-socket joint combines great strength with some mobility. The ball of the thigh bone is at an angle to the shaft so as to come more directly under the middle of the body.

THE KNEE
This joint works like a hinge, its main movements being forwards and backwards. It cannot cope with too much twisting, when it may become damaged.

THE ANKLE
Seven bones make up the ankle, a composite joint. Each bone moves a little in relation to its neighbours, giving great overall strength with limited flexibility.

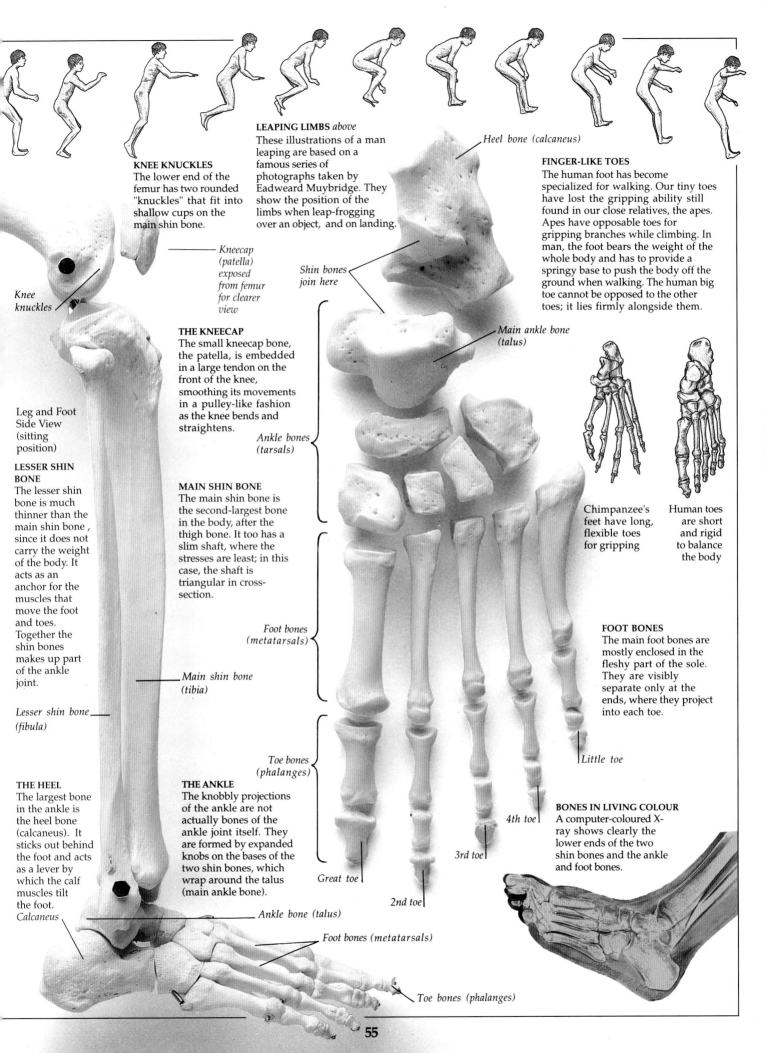

KNEE KNUCKLES
The lower end of the femur has two rounded "knuckles" that fit into shallow cups on the main shin bone.

Kneecap (patella) exposed from femur for clearer view

LEAPING LIMBS *above*
These illustrations of a man leaping are based on a famous series of photographs taken by Eadweard Muybridge. They show the position of the limbs when leap-frogging over an object, and on landing.

Heel bone (calcaneus)

FINGER-LIKE TOES
The human foot has become specialized for walking. Our tiny toes have lost the gripping ability still found in our close relatives, the apes. Apes have opposable toes for gripping branches while climbing. In man, the foot bears the weight of the whole body and has to provide a springy base to push the body off the ground when walking. The human big toe cannot be opposed to the other toes; it lies firmly alongside them.

Knee knuckles

Shin bones join here

THE KNEECAP
The small kneecap bone, the patella, is embedded in a large tendon on the front of the knee, smoothing its movements in a pulley-like fashion as the knee bends and straightens.

Main ankle bone (talus)

Ankle bones (tarsals)

Chimpanzee's feet have long, flexible toes for gripping

Human toes are short and rigid to balance the body

Leg and Foot Side View (sitting position)

LESSER SHIN BONE
The lesser shin bone is much thinner than the main shin bone, since it does not carry the weight of the body. It acts as an anchor for the muscles that move the foot and toes. Together the shin bones makes up part of the ankle joint.

MAIN SHIN BONE
The main shin bone is the second-largest bone in the body, after the thigh bone. It too has a slim shaft, where the stresses are least; in this case, the shaft is triangular in cross-section.

Main shin bone (tibia)

Foot bones (metatarsals)

FOOT BONES
The main foot bones are mostly enclosed in the fleshy part of the sole. They are visibly separate only at the ends, where they project into each toe.

Lesser shin bone (fibula)

Toe bones (phalanges)

Little toe

THE HEEL
The largest bone in the ankle is the heel bone (calcaneus). It sticks out behind the foot and acts as a lever by which the calf muscles tilt the foot.
Calcaneus

THE ANKLE
The knobbly projections of the ankle are not actually bones of the ankle joint itself. They are formed by expanded knobs on the bases of the two shin bones, which wrap around the talus (main ankle bone).

4th toe

3rd toe

BONES IN LIVING COLOUR
A computer-coloured X-ray shows clearly the lower ends of the two shin bones and the ankle and foot bones.

Ankle bone (talus)

Foot bones (metatarsals)

Great toe

2nd toe

Toe bones (phalanges)

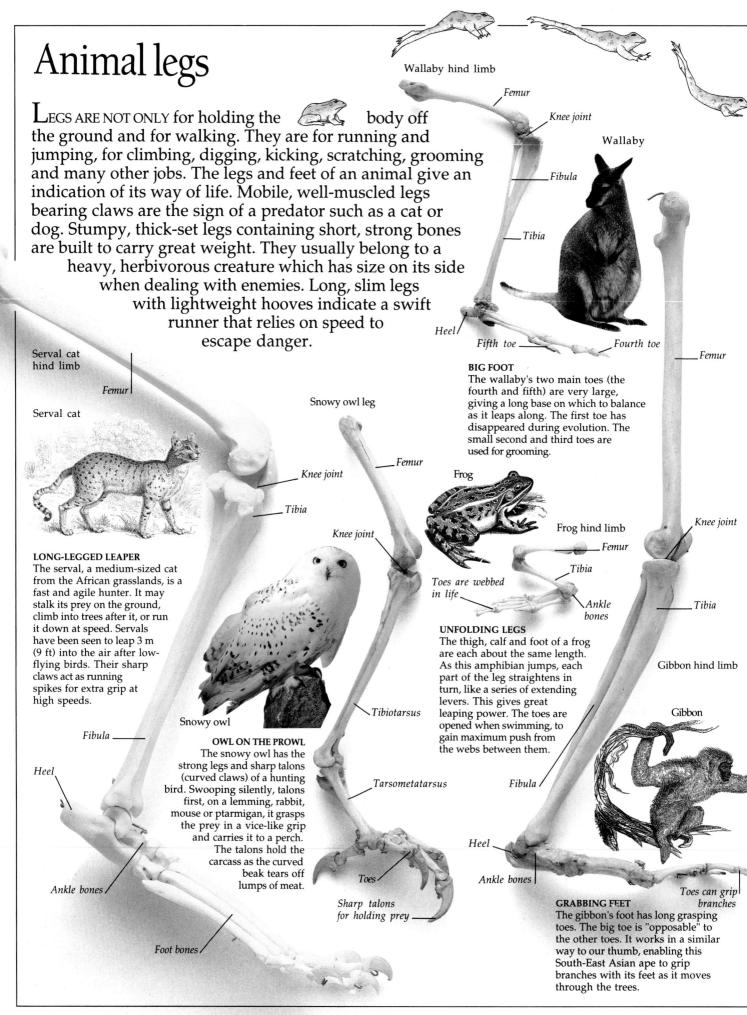

Animal legs

LEGS ARE NOT ONLY for holding the body off the ground and for walking. They are for running and jumping, for climbing, digging, kicking, scratching, grooming and many other jobs. The legs and feet of an animal give an indication of its way of life. Mobile, well-muscled legs bearing claws are the sign of a predator such as a cat or dog. Stumpy, thick-set legs containing short, strong bones are built to carry great weight. They usually belong to a heavy, herbivorous creature which has size on its side when dealing with enemies. Long, slim legs with lightweight hooves indicate a swift runner that relies on speed to escape danger.

Wallaby hind limb

Femur

Knee joint

Wallaby

Fibula

Tibia

Heel

Fifth toe

Fourth toe

Femur

BIG FOOT
The wallaby's two main toes (the fourth and fifth) are very large, giving a long base on which to balance as it leaps along. The first toe has disappeared during evolution. The small second and third toes are used for grooming.

Serval cat hind limb

Femur

Serval cat

Snowy owl leg

Femur

Knee joint

Tibia

Frog

Knee joint

Frog hind limb

Femur

Toes are webbed in life

Tibia

Ankle bones

LONG-LEGGED LEAPER
The serval, a medium-sized cat from the African grasslands, is a fast and agile hunter. It may stalk its prey on the ground, climb into trees after it, or run it down at speed. Servals have been seen to leap 3 m (9 ft) into the air after low-flying birds. Their sharp claws act as running spikes for extra grip at high speeds.

Fibula

Heel

Snowy owl

Tibiotarsus

OWL ON THE PROWL
The snowy owl has the strong legs and sharp talons (curved claws) of a hunting bird. Swooping silently, talons first, on a lemming, rabbit, mouse or ptarmigan, it grasps the prey in a vice-like grip and carries it to a perch. The talons hold the carcass as the curved beak tears off lumps of meat.

UNFOLDING LEGS
The thigh, calf and foot of a frog are each about the same length. As this amphibian jumps, each part of the leg straightens in turn, like a series of extending levers. This gives great leaping power. The toes are opened when swimming, to gain maximum push from the webs between them.

Femur

Knee joint

Tibia

Gibbon hind limb

Gibbon

Fibula

Tarsometatarsus

Ankle bones

Heel

Ankle bones

Heel

Toes

Sharp talons for holding prey

Foot bones

Toes can grip branches

GRABBING FEET
The gibbon's foot has long grasping toes. The big toe is "opposable" to the other toes. It works in a similar way to our thumb, enabling this South-East Asian ape to grip branches with its feet as it moves through the trees.

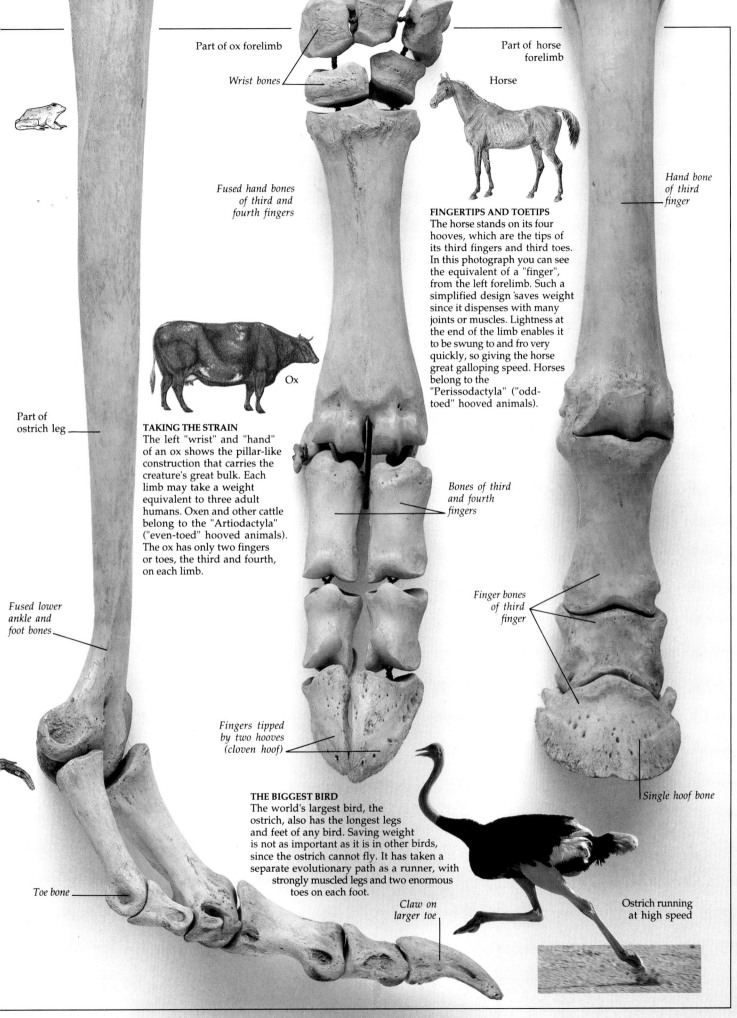

Part of ox forelimb

Part of horse forelimb

Wrist bones

Horse

Fused hand bones of third and fourth fingers

Hand bone of third finger

FINGERTIPS AND TOETIPS
The horse stands on its four hooves, which are the tips of its third fingers and third toes. In this photograph you can see the equivalent of a "finger", from the left forelimb. Such a simplified design saves weight since it dispenses with many joints or muscles. Lightness at the end of the limb enables it to be swung to and fro very quickly, so giving the horse great galloping speed. Horses belong to the "Perissodactyla" ("odd-toed" hooved animals).

Ox

Part of ostrich leg

TAKING THE STRAIN
The left "wrist" and "hand" of an ox shows the pillar-like construction that carries the creature's great bulk. Each limb may take a weight equivalent to three adult humans. Oxen and other cattle belong to the "Artiodactyla" ("even-toed" hooved animals). The ox has only two fingers or toes, the third and fourth, on each limb.

Bones of third and fourth fingers

Finger bones of third finger

Fused lower ankle and foot bones

Fingers tipped by two hooves (cloven hoof)

Single hoof bone

THE BIGGEST BIRD
The world's largest bird, the ostrich, also has the longest legs and feet of any bird. Saving weight is not as important as it is in other birds, since the ostrich cannot fly. It has taken a separate evolutionary path as a runner, with strongly muscled legs and two enormous toes on each foot.

Toe bone

Claw on larger toe

Ostrich running at high speed

The largest and smallest bones

Giant Hugo

BONES, LIKE OTHER PARTS OF THE BODY, vary in exact size and shape from person to person. Tall people have longer bones than shorter people, especially in the legs, where the thigh bone makes up about one-quarter of the body's height. Most of these variations in bone length are slight, however, with the average man being taller than the average woman. Occasionally, a disease or inherited condition affects development of bones as the baby grows in the womb. Or bone growth during childhood, which is controlled mainly by hormones, may be affected by disease, illness or a poor diet. The result is an unusually tall or small person.

Reconstructed fossil skeleton of Iguanodon

ANIMAL GIANTS
Dinosaurs, the largest land animals ever, had gigantic bones. The thigh bone of this Iguanodon (p. 12) was 1.3 m (4 ft 3 in) long. Some dinosaur arm bones were nearly 3 m (9 ft) long!

VERY TALL
Gigantism is caused by a hormone condition that makes the bones grow very fast. Authentic records give the tallest man ever as American Robert Wadlow at 2.7 m (8 ft 11 in). Above is another famous American, Giant Hugo.

VERY SMALL
The smallest humans measure about 60 cm to 75 cm (2 ft to 2 ft 6 in). One of the best-known midgets, shown here with his midget wife, was Charles Stratton ("General Tom Thumb") who was 1.02 m (3 ft 4 in) short.

"Tom Thumb" at his wedding

The size of the thighs

This array of ten thigh bones (femurs) shows the enormous size differences within the mammal group. In general, fast-moving animals have long, slender leg bones in relation to their body size. The seal's femurs are a special case: they are within the body, and this animal swims using its back flippers, which contain its shin and feet bones.

SHEEP *left*
Body length - 1.4 m (4 ft 8 in)
Femur length - 18 cm (7 in)

RABBIT
Body length - 30 cm (12 in)
Femur length - 8 cm (3 in)

HEDGEHOG
Body length - 20 cm (8 in)
Femur length - 4 cm (1.6 in)

SEAL
Body length - 1.6 m (5 ft)
Femur length - 11 cm (4.5 in)

DOG (BASSET HOUND)
Body length - 70 cm (2 ft 4 in)
Femur length - 11 cm (4.5 in)

CAT *left*
Body length - 50 cm (1 ft 8 in)
Femur length - 12 cm (5 in)

ROE DEER *right*
Body length - 1 m (3 ft)
Femur length - 18 cm (7 in)

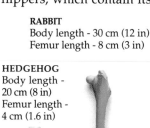

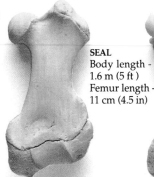

The smallest bones in the body

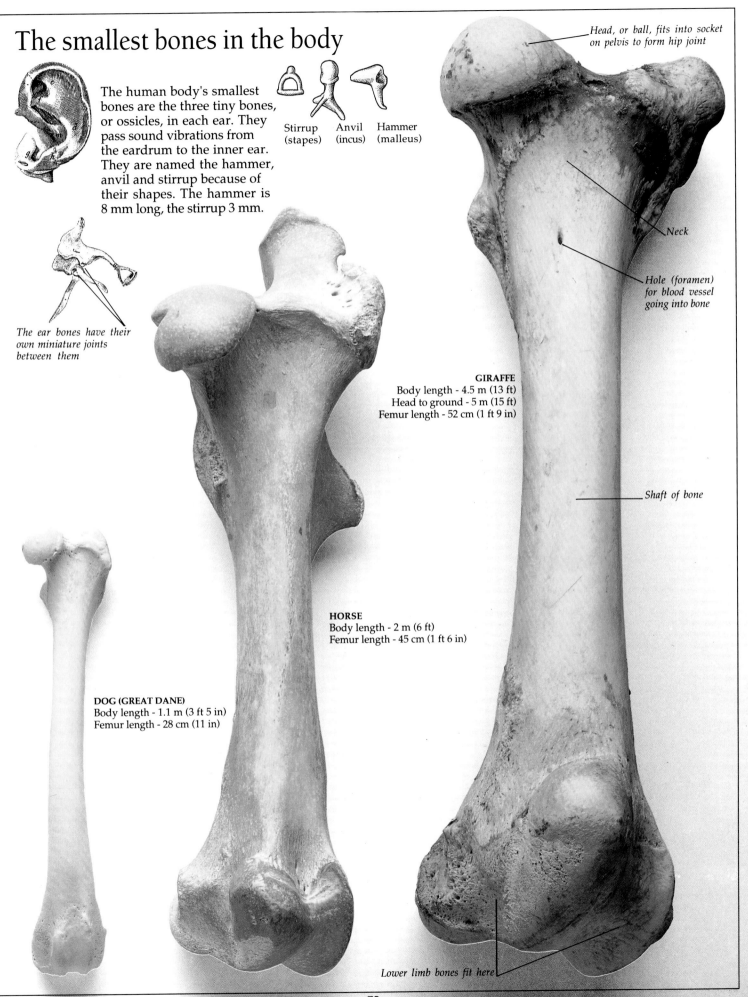

The human body's smallest bones are the three tiny bones, or ossicles, in each ear. They pass sound vibrations from the eardrum to the inner ear. They are named the hammer, anvil and stirrup because of their shapes. The hammer is 8 mm long, the stirrup 3 mm.

Stirrup (stapes)   Anvil (incus)   Hammer (malleus)

The ear bones have their own miniature joints between them

Head, or ball, fits into socket on pelvis to form hip joint

Neck

Hole (foramen) for blood vessel going into bone

GIRAFFE
Body length - 4.5 m (13 ft)
Head to ground - 5 m (15 ft)
Femur length - 52 cm (1 ft 9 in)

Shaft of bone

HORSE
Body length - 2 m (6 ft)
Femur length - 45 cm (1 ft 6 in)

DOG (GREAT DANE)
Body length - 1.1 m (3 ft 5 in)
Femur length - 28 cm (11 in)

Lower limb bones fit here

Structure and repair of bones

LIVING BONES ARE NOT PALE, dry and brittle, as they are in a museum case. Bone in the body is a busy living tissue. It is one-third water; it has blood vessels going in and out of it, supplying oxygen and nutrients and taking away wastes; certain bones contain marrow which produces blood cells; and bones have nerves that can feel pressure and pain. Bone is also a mineral store, containing calcium and other chemicals which give it hardness and rigidity. However, bone will give up its minerals in times of shortage, when other parts of the body (such as nerves) need them more. Bone tissue is made and maintained by several types of cells. "Osteoblasts" make new bone by hardening the protein collagen with minerals. "Osteocytes" maintain bone, passing nutrients and wastes back and forth between the blood and bone tissues. "Osteoclasts" destroy bone, releasing the minerals into the blood. All through life, bone is continually being reconstructed and reshaped as a result of the stresses, bends and breaks it endures.

ISOTOPE SCAN
Radioactive isotopes concentrate in bone, and a scan shows their distribution in the skeleton.

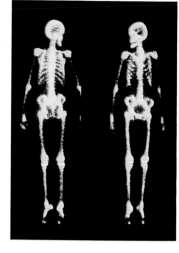

LIVING BONE
There are many ways of looking at living bones besides X-rays. By means of a scintillating crystal, this "scintigram" detects the concentrations of a radioactive isotope, which is injected into the body and taken up by bone tissue.

Inside bone

Bones are living examples of the engineer's art of design. Most bones have an outer "shell" of hard, solid, ivory-like "compact bone". Tendons, ligaments and other parts attach to this rigid shell via the living bone's "skin", the "periosteum". Inside the compact bone is a looser, lighter network of "spongy bone", that contains the marrow.

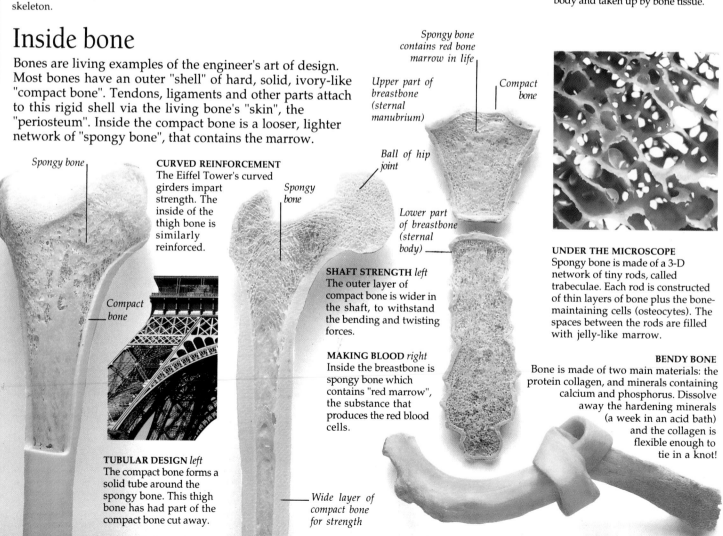

Spongy bone

CURVED REINFORCEMENT
The Eiffel Tower's curved girders impart strength. The inside of the thigh bone is similarly reinforced.

Compact bone

TUBULAR DESIGN *left*
The compact bone forms a solid tube around the spongy bone. This thigh bone has had part of the compact bone cut away.

Spongy bone

SHAFT STRENGTH *left*
The outer layer of compact bone is wider in the shaft, to withstand the bending and twisting forces.

MAKING BLOOD *right*
Inside the breastbone is spongy bone which contains "red marrow", the substance that produces the red blood cells.

Wide layer of compact bone for strength

Spongy bone contains red bone marrow in life

Upper part of breastbone (sternal manubrium)

Compact bone

Ball of hip joint

Lower part of breastbone (sternal body)

UNDER THE MICROSCOPE
Spongy bone is made of a 3-D network of tiny rods, called trabeculae. Each rod is constructed of thin layers of bone plus the bone-maintaining cells (osteocytes). The spaces between the rods are filled with jelly-like marrow.

BENDY BONE
Bone is made of two main materials: the protein collagen, and minerals containing calcium and phosphorus. Dissolve away the hardening minerals (a week in an acid bath) and the collagen is flexible enough to tie in a knot!

Breaks and mends

Since bone is an active living tissue, it can usually mend itself after a crack or break (fracture). The gap is bridged first by fibre-like material, to form a scar or callus. Then bone-making cells (osteoblasts) gradually move into the callus and harden it into true bone. This is usually a little lumpy around the edges, so bone-destroying cells (osteoclasts) sculpt the bumps to produce a smooth mend.

FROM BREAK TO MEND
Broken bones mend mainly in response to stresses. A dog broke its two forearm bones (below). The main weight-bearing bone mended well; the other, which carried hardly any weight, never really knitted together.

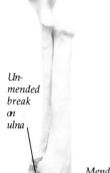

Un-mended break on ulna

Mended break on radius

ON THE MEND *right*
The X-rays show a broken humerus. It took several months to mend.

HELPING THE HEALING
Some broken bones need a "helping hand" to steady them in place, while the parts knit securely. In the past, a splint was the answer. Nowadays surgeons can use an "internal splint" - a plate of stainless steel screwed into place (below).

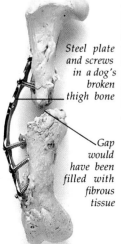

Steel plate and screws in a dog's broken thigh bone

Gap would have been filled with fibrous tissue

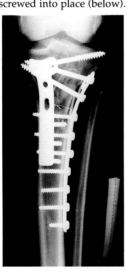

Day of break (top)

Several months later (below)

Right side of pelvis largely undamaged

Vertebrae fused into pelvis

New bone formed to strengthen twisted lower part of the pelvis

New socket worn for thigh bone

Cow's damaged pelvis

BROKEN PELVIS
This cow's pelvis was broken during a fall. The ball-shaped end of the thigh bone was pushed into a new position; the pelvis bone responded by making a new socket. The break healed naturally, but the cow then walked with a limp.

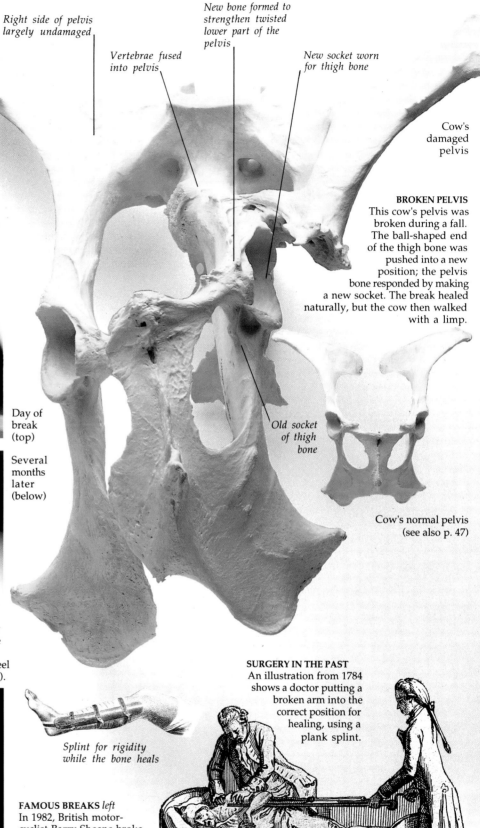

Old socket of thigh bone

Cow's normal pelvis (see also p. 47)

SURGERY IN THE PAST
An illustration from 1784 shows a doctor putting a broken arm into the correct position for healing, using a plank splint.

Splint for rigidity while the bone heals

FAMOUS BREAKS *left*
In 1982, British motor-cyclist Barry Sheene broke both legs in several places in a 250 kph (160 mph) crash. This X-ray shows some of the 26 screws and plates that were used to piece the shattered bones back together. Soon Sheene was walking - and riding - again.

Glossary of bone names

ALL THE BONES IN the human body have names. Doctors and other experts use very precise terms, mainly derived from Latin or Greek. This allows them to refer to the exact bone. Bones also have more general names, and a mixture of specific and general terms is normally used when we are talking about them. The number of bones in the adult human body is around 200 to 210, depending on exactly how you count them (is the pelvis one, two or six bones?) The usual number given is 206. Some people have extra or fewer ribs, extra "sutural bones" in the skull, or other variations. A developing baby has more than 300 bones, some of which fuse together during infancy and childhood.

Forehead *Frontal bone*
Nose bone *Nasal* (2)
Cheek *Zygoma* (2)
Upper jaw *Maxilla* (2)
Teeth (32)
Lower jaw *Mandible*

Collar bone *Clavicle* (2)

Manubrium
Sternal body
Xiphoid process
Breastbone *Sternum* (3 parts)

Costal cartilage

Upper-arm bone (2) *Humerus*

Main forearm bone (2) *Radius*

Lesser forearm bone (2) *Ulna*

Ilium
Ischium
Pubis
Hip bone *Pelvis* (6 fused bones)

Thigh bone (2) *Femur*

Kneecap (2) *Patella*

Main shin bone (2) *Tibia*

Calf bone (2) *Fibula*

Front view

Foot

Bones of the hand

Index finger
Middle finger
Ring finger
Little finger

Distal phalanx
Middle phalanx
Proximal phalanx
Finger bones *Phalanges*

Thumb

Fifth metacarpal

Hand (palm) bones (5 in each hand) *Metacarpals*

Trapezium

Wrist bones (8 in each hand) *Carpals*

Pisiform

Triquetral

Hamate

Lunate

Trapezoid

Capitate

Scaphoid

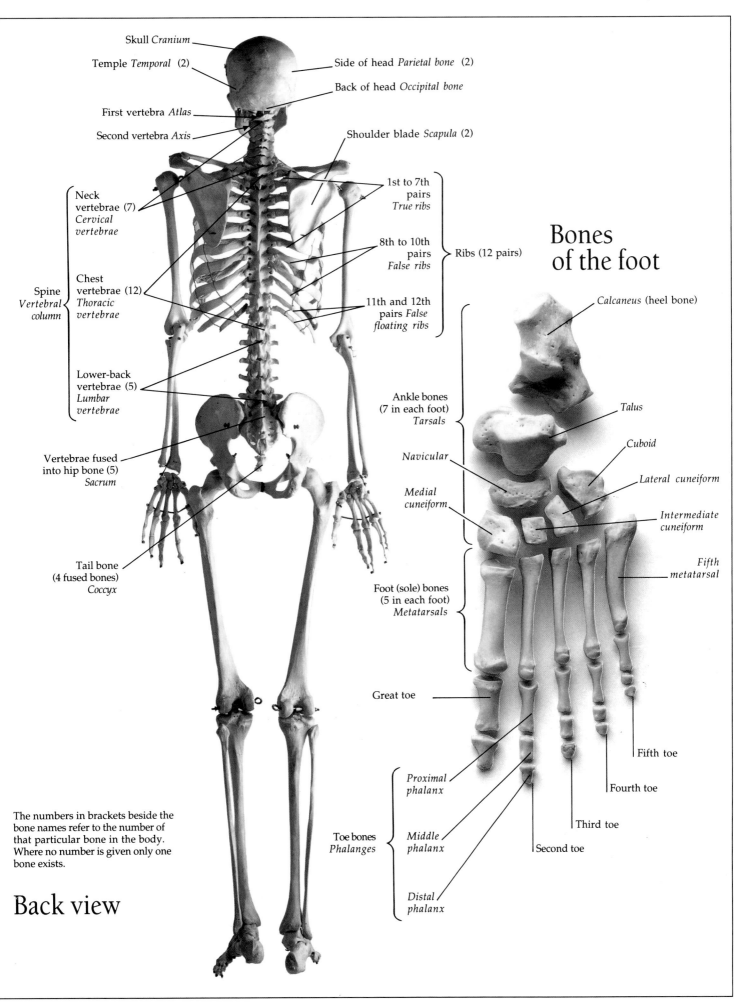

Skull *Cranium*

Temple *Temporal* (2)

Side of head *Parietal bone* (2)

Back of head *Occipital bone*

First vertebra *Atlas*

Second vertebra *Axis*

Shoulder blade *Scapula* (2)

Neck
vertebrae (7)
*Cervical
vertebrae*

1st to 7th
pairs
True ribs

8th to 10th
pairs
False ribs

Ribs (12 pairs)

Spine
*Vertebral
column*

Chest
vertebrae (12)
*Thoracic
vertebrae*

11th and 12th
pairs *False
floating ribs*

Bones
of the foot

Calcaneus (heel bone)

Ankle bones
(7 in each foot)
Tarsals

Talus

Cuboid

Navicular

Lateral cuneiform

Lower-back
vertebrae (5)
*Lumbar
vertebrae*

*Medial
cuneiform*

*Intermediate
cuneiform*

Vertebrae fused
into hip bone (5)
Sacrum

*Fifth
metatarsal*

Foot (sole) bones
(5 in each foot)
Metatarsals

Tail bone
(4 fused bones)
Coccyx

Great toe

Fifth toe

Fourth toe

Third toe

The numbers in brackets beside the
bone names refer to the number of
that particular bone in the body.
Where no number is given only one
bone exists.

*Proximal
phalanx*

Toe bones
Phalanges

*Middle
phalanx*

Second toe

Back view

*Distal
phalanx*

Did you know?

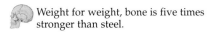

FASCINATING FACTS

Weight for weight, bone is five times stronger than steel.

Compact bone is the second hardest material in the body. The hardest is tooth enamel.

People who are "double jointed" do not actually have extra joints, they just have looser ligaments.

Some people have extra tiny bones, called sesamoid bones, that grow within their tendons. These bones most often form in the hands and feet.

If a lizard loses its tail, it can grow a new one. In fact, the bones in a lizard's tail have special break points designed to fracture easily if the lizard is caught. The twitching, severed tail then distracts the predator, allowing the rest of the lizard to escape.

Three-stages in the regrowth of a lizard's tail

Sharks, rays and skates do not have any bones at all, instead their skeletons are made up entirely of cartilage.

When a person has a badly fractured bone that will not heal, surgeons can sometimes take bone chips from the pelvis and place them in the break. The chips soon grow to fill the gaps and heal the bone.

The axolotl, a type of salamander, is able to grow new legs and a new tail after a predator attack. It can even grow back some of its feathery external gills.

Some owls' ears are at different levels. Each ear picks up a sound at a slightly different time, allowing pinpoint accuracy of the sound's direction.

The Native American Blackfeet and Dakota tribes used to paint the skulls of buffalo and decorate them with sage and grass as part of their ritual Sun Dance.

The base of a coral reef is made up of the calcium-rich skeletal remains of millions of tiny coral animals. The longest reef in the world is the Great Barrier Reef in Australia, which stretches for about 2,010 km (1,250 miles).

Contrary to popular belief, men and women have exactly the same number of ribs.

When a child grows, bones such as the thigh bone (femur) do not grow evenly from all points along their length. Instead, they grow only from their ends.

In a fall, a baby is less likely to break a bone than an adult. This is partly because a baby is lighter than an adult, but mostly it is because a baby's bones are not yet fully formed. A baby's skeleton has a lot of soft, flexible cartilage that will slowly turn into hard bone as the child grows.

Both sharks and crocodiles are continually growing sharp new teeth. When they catch prey, they often break or lose teeth, but new ones soon grow to replace them. A shark may grow more than 20,000 teeth in its lifetime.

Horn, a core of bone surrounded by horn protein (keratin)

A buffalo skull specially painted to be placed at an altar in the Blackfeet Sun Dance.

Over half the bones in a human are in the wrists, hands, ankles and feet.

Horn is made up of many compressed hair fibres, and hair is made from the structural protein keratin, which also forms nails and feathers.

Around one fifth (20%) of a person's total body weight comes from just the bones and teeth.

Most people have 12 pairs of ribs, however, five per cent of the population is born with one or more extra ribs. Some people, on the other hand, have only 11 pairs of ribs.

Orca (killer whale) skeleton

Chevrons, V-shaped bones where muscles join the backbone.

An orca, or killer whale, swims using its powerful tail. Although it has no back legs, many whales do have a few vestigial (small unused) leg bones, indicating that their ancestors once walked on land.

In order to avoid weak and brittle bones in older age, it is important to do weight-bearing exercise, such as walking, and to eat a healthy diet that includes plenty of calcium when you are young. Calcium-rich foods include milk, yogurt, broccoli, spinach, hard cheese, tofu, and canned sardines and salmon.

A cuttlefish "bone", such as those used by pet birds to sharpen their beaks, is in fact the living cuttlefish's internal shell. As well as providing structural support, the shell helps the animal move about. The cuttlefish fills the many tiny air spaces within the shell with gas to make itself rise, and then replaces the gas with fluid to make itself sink.

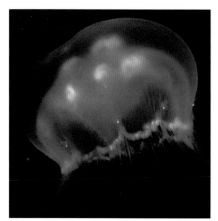

Jellyfish swim by expanding and contracting their bodies.

Some jellyfish can grow to 2 m (6 ft 6 in) long, and yet they have neither an external nor an internal skeleton: they get all the support they need from the surrounding seawater.

In the same way that humans lose their baby teeth as they grow up, young elephants lose their milk tusks when they are about one year old.

A single molar (grinding tooth) from an adult elephant weighs about 4.5 kg (10 lb). That's heavier than a brick.

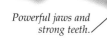

Powerful jaws and strong teeth.

By examining a skull, forensic scientists can work out what its owner may have looked like when alive. With use of either clay models or computer programs, they can build up the person's features based on the shapes of the bones. This method is used both to work out the identity of long-dead murder victims and to study people from ancient cultures.

Forensic scientists are now able to extract DNA, a chemical found in all body cells, from the skeleton of a murder victim. This can enable them to work out the identity of a long-dead victim from just one small piece of bone or other tissue from any part of the body.

Fossil of *Sparnodus*, a fish that lived about 55 million years ago.

The word *petrify* actually means to turn a once-living plant or animal into stone. Some fossils are formed when minerals dissolved in water flow into the gaps in buried bones, slowly strengthening the bone and turning it into solid, long-lasting rock.

Record Breakers

Giraffe

A giraffe has only seven neck bones, the same number as a human.

TALLEST LIVING LAND ANIMAL
Giraffes have the tallest skeleton of any living land animal. They can reach 6 m (19½ ft), as tall as three adult men.

LARGEST SKELETON
The blue whale has the largest skeleton of any living animal. It measures about 33.5 m (110 ft) in length.

LONGEST REPTILE SKELETON
The saltwater crocodile's skeleton can reach a length of 10 m (33 ft).

SMALLEST BIRD SKELETON
The tiny skeleton of the male bee hummingbird grows to only about 5.7 cm (2¼ in) in length. That's not much bigger than many moths.

LARGEST SPIDER SKELETON
The exoskeleton of the enormous goliath bird-eating spider from South America can reach a width of up to 28 cm (11 in) across the span of its legs.

LARGEST CRUSTACEAN
The exoskeleton of the Japanese spider crab can reach a width of up to 4 m (13 ft) across the span of its claws.

LARGEST FOSSIL BIRD
The wing bones of *Argentavis magnificens*, a prehistoric bird, spanned 7.6 m (25 ft).

LARGEST FOSSIL INSECT
The largest prehistoric insect on record is the 300-million-year-old dragonfly, *Meganeura monyi*. Its wings could span up to 75 cm (29½ in).

Did you know? (continued)

Q Why does a hermit crab live inside a mollusc shell?

A Unlike most crabs, the hermit crab does not have a hard outer shell on its abdomen. This makes it vulnerable to attack so it lives inside an old mollusc shell for protection. As it grows larger, it discards its cramped shell for a larger one.

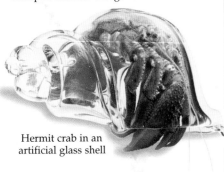

Hermit crab in an artificial glass shell

Q If bones don't bend, how can exercise make my body more flexible?

A Bones that meet at a joint are held in place by ligaments. Careful exercise can slowly stretch these ligaments, enabling the joints to have a greater range of movement.

Q Why doesn't a snake break the bones in its rib cage when it swallows a large animal whole?

A A snake has no breastbone, instead the ribs are joined by flexible muscles. Also, the joints in a snake's backbone are very loose, allowing the body to coil and bend in all directions.

Q Why do cats' "knees" bend backwards?

A The bones on a cat that are equivalent to a human's knees are high up near the abdomen. The joints that look like knees are actually the equivalent of our ankles, which is why they bend the other way. Cats usually walk on just their toes, which enables them to run very swiftly.

Q Why is regular exercise good for your bones?

A Exercise tones up your muscles, enabling them to hold the bones in their correct positions, preventing health problems such as backache and bad posture. Regular weight-bearing exercise, such as walking or running, also improves your bone mass: it helps increase the amount of calcium stored in your bones.

Q How does an insect move its hard exoskeleton?

A The hard plates that make up an insect's exoskeleton meet at flexible joints. Muscles, attached to the exoskeleton across the insides of these joints contract to produce movement; four different muscles pull each limb forwards, backwards, upwards and downwards.

Q Do worms have a skeleton?

A A worm does not have bones or cartilage, but it does have what is known as a hydrostatic skeleton. Its body is divided into separate segments, or cavities, that are filled with fluid. The fluid fills out the worm's body in a similar way that tap water can fill a balloon.

Q How do huge whales manage to find and eat krill and other minute sea creatures?

A A baleen whale, such as a right whale or a humpback whale, does not have teeth. Instead, it has rows of fringed plates that hang inside its mouth and filter food from the sea water. Like human hair and nails, the plates are made of the protein keratin, although they are sometimes inaccurately referred to as "whalebone".

Q Do whales have tusks?

A Most whales don't have tusks, but the male narwhal whale, which lives in remote parts of the arctic and subarctic, usually has one very long spiralling ivory tusk that can reach as long as 2.4 m (8 ft). Some people believe that narwhal tusks washed up on the seashore may have given rise to the unicorn myth.

A hoverfly

Q Why does the hoverfly have black and yellow stripes like a wasp?

A Some harmless insects, such as the hoverfly, protect themselves by mimicking the appearance of dangerous ones. The stingless hoverfly's exoskeleton resembles that of a wasp so that predators, such as birds, will leave it alone.

Q How do X-ray machines see through skin to the bones?

A X-ray machines fire out a beam of invisible rays. These rays can travel straight through skin and other soft body tissue, but not bone. When a piece of photographic film is placed behind the body, the X-rays go through the soft tissue and expose the film, turning it a darker colour. The denser bones act like a stencil, preventing the rays reaching the film directly behind them. They leave behind a white unexposed image of the bones' shapes.

The spiralling tusk on a male narwhal

Male narwhal whale

Q Do our bones have any other roles apart from supporting the body?

A Yes, both our red and white blood cells are made inside the bones. The red blood cells carry oxygen around the body and the white ones destroy disease-causing organisms such as bacteria and viruses.

Q How does a spider moult its exoskeleton?

A Before each moult, a spider partially digests and absorbs the old exoskeleton, preserving minerals and starting to break it down. Lubricating fluid between the old and new cuticle then helps the spider shed the old skin, revealing the new one. The new skeleton stays soft for a short time, allowing the spider to grow.

Tarantula moult

Q Why do flatfish, such as flounder, have both their eyes on the same side of their head?

A The skeletons of flatfish have adapted to allow these animals to live on the seabed. Their flat shape prevents being seen by predators and prey, alike. Both their eyes are on the upward-facing side of the body, and they also have a special cavity in their flat skeleton to allow for the heart and other organs.

Q Do animals with beaks have teeth?

A Birds do not have teeth as the weight of teeth would make their skeleton too heavy for flight. Some beaked marine animals, however, do have teeth. The common dolphin, for example, has about 50 pairs of teeth in its upper and lower jaws. It uses them to grip food, which it swallows whole.

Q Why are bones breakable?

A Because our bones are hollow, they break more easily than they would if they were solid all the way through. However, if our bones were solid, our skeleton would be too heavy for us to carry or move about.

Q Why do some animals have eyes that face forwards, while other have eyes that point in opposite directions.

A Predatory animals (animal that hunt) often have two forward facing eyes. This gives them a wide field of binocular vision, which is three-dimensional and enables them to pinpoint prey very accurately. Animals that are hunted, on the other hand, often have eyes that point in opposite directions. This enables them to look for danger all around and above themselves without needing to turn their head.

Q Why are the exoskeletons of beetles and other insects so colourful?

A Often the only visible part of animals such as beetles and other insects is their exoskeleton. Some poisonous beetles are brightly coloured to warm potential prey not to eat them. Other beetles are coloured green or brown to blend in with surrounding plant matter and avoid being seen by predators.

Q What is the difference between tusks and teeth?

A There is no real difference: tusks are teeth that project beyond the jaw. A walrus's tusks are elongated canine teeth, and an elephant's tusks are elongated incisors.

Q Is the part of a horse's hoof that we can see really its toe bone?

A No, the hoof surrounds and protects the fragile toe or finger bones. When the horse is alive, a pad of fat lies between the bones and the hoof to act as a shock-absorber.

A horse's toe bones sit inside the hoof.

Sleeping budgerigar

Q Why don't birds fall off their perches when they get tired or sleep?

A When a bird perches on a branch, it bends its legs and rests its weight on the bones in its feet. This pulls the leg tendons tight, clamping the toes around the branch. To release its grip, the bird must contract its toe muscles.

Male moose with antlers

Q What is the difference between horns and antlers?

A True horns are simple, unbranched structures that are never shed. They are composed of a bony core surrounded by a softer, outer layer of horn protein (keratin). Horns are found on cattle, sheep, goats and antelopes. Antlers, on the other hand, are branched structures that are shed and regrown. They are composed entirely of bone, and in life, they are covered with a furry, velvet-like skin. They are found on elk, including moose, and deer.

Find out more

IF YOU ARE INTERESTED in finding out more about skeletons, there are plenty of different ways you can do so. One of the most interesting options is to visit a museum (see some suggestions, right). Most natural history museums are packed with skeletons of everything from spiders to dinosaurs. Many science museums have interactive exhibits that allow you to hold and investigate model bones, seeing for yourself how they fit together and move. Some historical museums display the skeletons of ancient peoples, along with other artifacts such as clothing, household implements and tools.

Other ways you can find out more about skeletons include searching the internet (see below) and investigating the books, CD-ROMs and videos at your local library. You might even want to find out about possible careers that involve working with bones, such as palaeontology or physiotherapy.

A PALAEONTOLOGIST AT WORK
A palaeontologist is a scientist who studies the bones of fossils, such as dinosaurs. Many palaeonotologists work in museums, where funding for public displays helps pay for their research. When museum visitors see a dinosaur on display, they are seeing the final results of years of planning and hard work.

MUSEUM
This museum technician is using a pair of callipers to measure the jaw of a bottle-nosed dolphin. The information she collects may be used to help construct models of the dolphin for display in the museum. Once her work is completed, the bones themselves may be put on display in the museum for visitors to view.

A physiotherapist using a skeleton to help discuss a patient's condition.

A *T. rex* skeleton at the American Museum of Natural History in New York

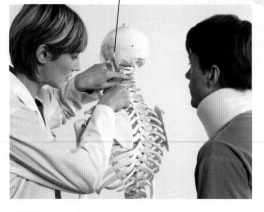

BONES AND MEDICINE
The first time many of us become aware of our bones is when we have a health problem. Physiotherapists, doctors and many other health-care professionals have studied the human skeleton in detail and can often answer any questions we may have.

USEFUL WEBSITES

- A health-based site with information about the human skeleton:
  www.innerbody.com/htm/body.html

- A fun site that allows visitors to view, compare and read about the bones of a human, a gorilla and a baboon:
  www.eskeletons.org

- An interesting website featuring the largest *T. rex* ever found:
  www.fmnh.org/sue

- This BBC website has useful information on bones for children:
  www.bbc.co.uk/education/health/kids/bones.shtml

- A site about human and animal skeletons for young children:
  www.enchantedlearning.com/themes/skeleton.shtml

- An American educational site with a fun quiz for children of about 10 years of age:
  www.kidport.com/grade5/science/bodybones.htm

STUDYING BONES

Children often learn about bones in science class. Older children and adults can learn more about them by choosing to study biology. Medical students learn even more in anatomy class, in which they study the structure of the body in detail.

MODEL MAKING

A fun, hands-on way to really understand how bones fit together is to construct a model skeleton. Science supply shops, craft shops and toy stores often sell kits of human, dinosaur or other skeletons. They come in varying complexities to suit all ages and purposes.

Model skeleton constructed out of paper

Places to visit

THE NATURAL HISTORY MUSEUM
Cromwell Road
London SW7 5BD

THE SCIENCE MUSEUM
Exhibition Road
London SW7

AMERICAN MUSEUM OF NATURAL HISTORY
Central Park West and 79th Street
New York, New York

NATURAL HISTORY MUSEUM OF LOS ANGELES COUNTY
900 Exposition Boulevard
Los Angeles CA 90007

THE FIELD MUSEUM
1400 South Lake Shore Drive
Chicago IL 60605

ROYAL TYRRELL MUSEUM OF PALAEONTOLOGY
Drumheller
Alberta J0J OY0
   Canada

THE AUSTRALIAN MUSEUM
6 College Street Sydney
New South Wales 2010
Australia

Lion skull

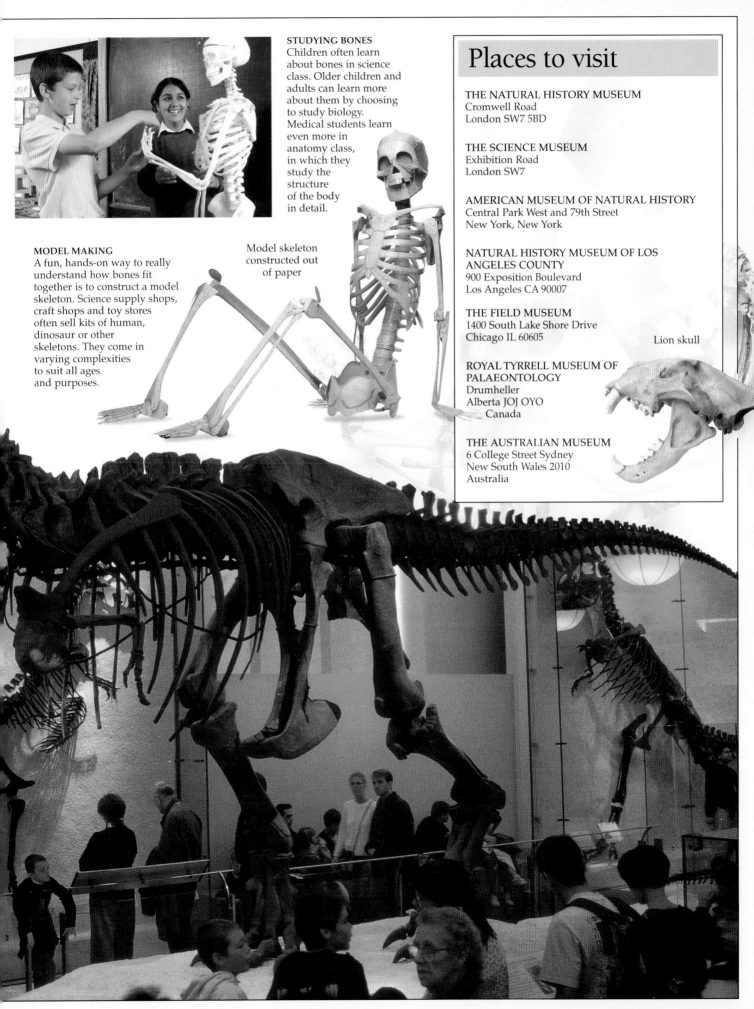

Glossary

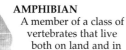

Human backbone

AMPHIBIAN
A member of a class of vertebrates that live both on land and in water, such as a frog.

ARACHNID
A member of a class of arthropods with four pairs of legs, such as a spider or a scorpion.

ARTHROPOD
A member of the arthropoda division of the animal kingdom. They have a segmented exoskeleton with jointed legs. Arachnids, insects, crustacea, millipedes and centipedes are all examples of arthropods.

BACKBONE
A strong, flexible chain of bones that runs the length of the body in humans and many other animals. It is also known as the spine or vertebral column.

BONE
A hard body tissue that gives strength to the skeleton. In humans and many animals, it is composed of outer compact bone and inner spongy bone and bone marrow.

CANINE TOOTH
A pointed tooth, usually next to the incisors, that grips and pierces food.

CARNASSIAL TOOTH
A specialized tooth on a carnivore that is adapted for tearing meat. Most carnassial teeth are large and long.

CARNIVORE
An animal that eats mainly meat.

CARPAL
Vertebrate wrist bone.

Hand X-rays showing the replacement of cartilage with bone as a person grows.

Cartilage   Bone

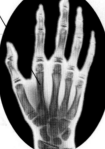

CARTILAGE
A tough, flexible substance that protects vertebrate joints. It is sometimes called gristle. Cartilaginous fish, such as sharks, have a skeleton made entirely of cartilage.

CHITIN
A light, strong, substance found in the exoskeletons of arthropods.

COLLAGEN
A connective protein that forms strong, elastic fibres. It is found found in bone and skin.

COMPACT BONE
The hard material that forms the outer layer of a bone.

CRANIUM
The part of the skull that surrounds the brain.

CRUSTACEAN
A member of a class of mainly aquatic arthropods, such as crab or lobster, with a hard case, or "crust", that encloses the body.

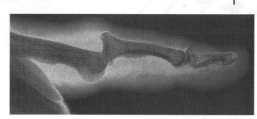

A dislocated finger bone

DENTINE
A hard substance beneath the enamel of vertebrate teeth. It is also known as ivory.

DISLOCATE
A movement that pulls or pushes a bone out of its place within a joint.

ECHINODERM
A marine invertebrate, such as a starfish, with a skeleton made up of hard, bony plates called ossicles.

ENAMEL
A tough substance that forms the outer coating of vertebrate teeth.

ENDOSKELETON
A hard skeleton found inside an animal's body.

EXOSKELETON
A hard skeleton outside of an animal's body.

FEMUR
Vertebrate thigh bone.

FONTANELLE
An area of cartilage in a baby's skull. It turns to bone as the baby grows.

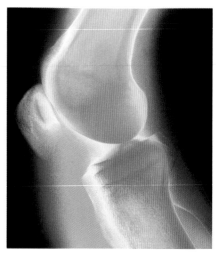

Artificially coloured X-ray of knee joint

FORENSIC SCIENCE
The analysis of skeletal or other material in regard to questions of civil or criminal law.

GEOLOGY
The science of the Earth's physical history and development.

HERBIVORE
An animal that eats mainly plants.

HYDROSTATIC SKELETON
An invertebrate skeleton maintained by the internal pressure of the body fluids.

INCISOR TOOTH
A chisel-shaped cutting tooth at the front of the mouth in vertebrates.

INVERTEBRATE
An animal that does not have a backbone.

JOINT
Any part of a skeleton where two or more bones meet.

KERATIN
A structural protein that forms strong, flexible fibres, and makes up horn, hair and nails.

KNUCKLE
A joint between the bones in a finger or thumb.

LIGAMENT
A strong, fibrous band of tissue that joins bones together at joints.

MANDIBLE
A vertebrate's lower jaw, or the biting mouthpart of an arthropod.

MARROW
A substance found within spongy bone. It is where blood cells are made.

MAXILLA Vertebrate upper jaw, or arthropod mouthpart to rear of the mandible.

MOLAR TOOTH
Chewing tooth at the back of a vertebrate jaw.

MOLLUSC
An invertebrate with a soft body that is usually covered by a hard shell. The group includes snails, oysters and scallops.

MOULT
The periodic shedding of an outer covering, such as an exoskeleton, fur or feathers, to allow for growth or seasonal change.

MUMMIFICATION
The process of drying and preserving either human or animal remains by natural or artificial means.

NOCTURNAL
An animal that is active at night.

OMNIVORE
An animal that eats both plant and other animal material.

OPPOSABLE
An opposable thumb (in humans) or big toes (in chimps and some other animals) is one that can be manipulated to touch, or oppose, the other fingers or toes on the same hand or foot. This enables the limb to be used for holding and manipulating objects.

ORBIT
A bony socket in which the eyeball is situated.

OSSICLE
Any small bone or other calcified structure, such as a plate in an echinoderm shell or an exoskeleton. In humans, it is used to refer to small bones within the ear.

OSSIFICATION
The process whereby cartilage turns into hard bone. In humans, some ossification continues to occur after birth.

PERIOSTEUM
A thin, strong membrane that covers the surface of bones, except at the joints.

PHALANGES
The bones of the fingers or toes in vertebrates, including humans.

PREMOLAR TOOTH
Vertebrate tooth that is situated in front of the molars.

PRONOTUM
Protective head shield in some insect exoskeletons.

REPTILE
A member of a class of vertebrates with scaly skin that lays sealed eggs. Snakes, lizards and crocodiles are all reptiles.

RODENT
A member of an order of mammals with continuously growing incisors that are kept the right size by the continuous gnawing. Rabbits and guinea pigs are both rodents.

SCAPULA
Vertebrate shoulder blade.

SEDIMENT
Mineral or organic matter carried and deposited by water, wind or ice.

SEDIMENTARY ROCK
Rock formed from layers of sediment.

SINUS
An air-filled hole in the skull. The sinuses around the nasal passages are filled with mucous-producing membranes.

SKELETON
A strong framework that supports the body and, in humans and some animals, provides attachment points for the muscles.

SPINAL CORD
The cord of nerve tissue enclosed and protected by the spinal column (backbone). These nerves connect the brain to the rest of the body.

SPONGY BONE
A honeycomb-like material in the interior of bones. It is filled with bone marrow.

STERNUM
Vertebrate breast bone.

SUTURE
An immovable joint between the individual bones in the skull that helps provide a strong protective casing.

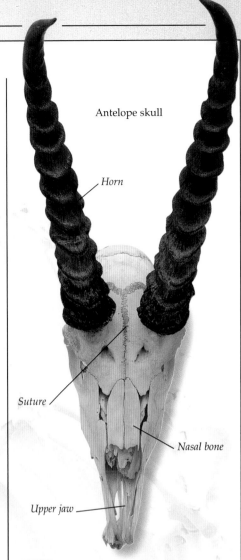

Antelope skull

Horn

Suture

Nasal bone

Upper jaw

TUSK
A vertebrate tooth that projects beyond the upper or lower jaw.

VERTEBRA
One of the bones make up the spinal column (backbone).

VERTEBRATE
An animal with a bony or cartilaginous spinal column (backbone).

Image of a human scapula

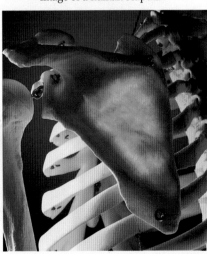

Flexible caudal (tail) fin

Pectoral fin

Vertebra

Cartilaginous dogfish skeleton

Index

Acknowledgements

Dorling Kindersley would like to thank:

The Booth Museum of Natural History, Brighton, Peter Gardiner, Griffin and George, The Royal College of Surgeons of England, The Royal Veterinary College, and Paul Vos for skeletal material.

Dr A.V. Mitchell for the X-rays.

Richard and Hilary Bird for the index.

Fred Ford and Mike Pilley of Radius Graphics, and Ray Owen and Nick Madren for artwork.

Anne-Marie Bulat for her work on the initial stages of the book.

Dave King for special photography on pages 14-20 and pages 32-3.

Picture credits
The publisher would like to thank the following for their kind permission to reproduce their images:

Position key: m=middle; b=bottom; l=left; r=right; t=top
American Museum of Natural History: 64tr.
Des and Jen Bartlett/Bruce Coleman Ltd: 51tl
Des and Jen Bartlett/Survival Anglia: 57b
Erwin and Peggy Baurer/Bruce Colema Ltd: 47t
BPCC/Aldus Archive: 9b, 10t, mr, br; 11t; 29b
Booth Museum of Natural History: 68 background.
Bridgeman Art Library: 8m; 9ml, 10ml; 11ml
Jane Burton/Bruce Coleman Ltd, 33m
A. Campbell/NHPA: 34b
CNRI/Science Photo Library: 26m; 49tr; 55br; 60tl
Bruce Coleman Ltd: 51br 67br.
A. Davies/NHPA: 34t
Elsdint/Science Photo Library: 60tl
Francisco Eriza/Bruce Coleman Ltd: 50b
FLPA - Images of nature:
Mark Newman 68-9b.
Jeff Foott/Survival Anglia: 50mr, 42m, 48m; 54m
John Freeman, London: 6bl; 7t;

Tom and Pam Gardener/Frank Lane Picture Agency: 33t
P. Boycolea/Alan Hutchinson Library: 11bl
Sonia Halliday Photographs: 43b
E. Hanumantha Rao/NHPA: 53b
Julian Hector/Planet Earth Pictures: 50t
T. Henshaw/Daily Telegraph Colour Library: 54br
Michael Holford: 9t; 11mr; 36t
Eric Hosking: 33br; 51bl; 42tr; 56m
F Jack Jackson/Planet Earth Pictures: 4l
Antony Joyce/Planet Earth Pictures, 33br
Gordon Langsbury/Bruce Coleman Ltd: 32tr
Michael Leach/NHPA: 56t
Mike Linley: 66tl
Lacz Lemoine/NHPA: 32mr
Mansell Collection: 6m; 7m; 15t; 36m; 43t; 56mr; 58t; 61br
Marineland/Frank Lane Picture Agency: 51m
Mary Evans Picture Libvrary: 6tl, br; 7b; 8t, b; 9mr; 10bl; 11br; 13br; 14l, r; 16ml; 26t; 45br; 58ml, mr; 62tl
Masterfile UK: 68bl; Dale Sanders 65cl.
Frieder Michler/Science Photo Library: 60m
Geoff Moon/Frank Lane Picture Agency: 32br
Alfred Pasieka/Bruce Coleman Ltd: 22t
Philip Perry/Frank Lane Picture Agency: 35t
The Natural History Museum, London: 66-7b; 68tr.
Oxford Scientific Films: Harold Taylor 66tr; M.A. Chappell 67tr.
Education Photos: 69tl.

Dieter and Mary Plage/Bruce Coleman Ltd: 40b
Hans Reinhard/Bruce Coleman Ltd: 32bl; 46bl
Leonard Lee Rue/Bruce Coleman Ltd: 32ml, 52ml
Keith Scholey/Planet Earth Pictures: 50ml
Johnathan Scott/Planet Earth Pictures: 37bl
Silvestris/Frank Lane Picture Agency: 35b
Syndication International: 61bl
Science Photo Library:
68c, 70tr, 70c, 70bl, 71br.
Terry Whittaker/Frank Lane Picture Agency: 52bl
ZEFA: 37t; 39tr; 60b
Gunter Ziesler/Bruce Coleman Ltd: 37 br

Illustrations by Will Giles: 12b; 13t, m; 27l, r; 28b; 29t, 34bl, m; 35tl, br; 37m; 38b, 39l, 52b; 44bl, bm, br; 45bl, bm; 46ml, mr, b; 47ml, bl, br, 48ml, 49m; 51tr, 52m, b; 53t, ml, mr; 54bm; 55m; 56t; 59m

Picture research by: Millie Trowbridge
All other images © Dorling Kindersley.
For further information see:
www.dkimages.com